TABLE OF CONTENTS

1. ASSESSING YOUR HOUSING NEEDS

A decision to search for a first home, to change homes, or to build or remodel opens the door to a challenging, perhaps frustrating, but exciting experience. This handbook has guidelines to help you sort through many factors, organize your thinking, and make decisions. It focuses on planning, because time spent in forethought saves money, frustration, and time later. Delays caused by changing your mind often are costly in materials and labor. Select carefully from the large number of alternatives at each stage, and then change a decision only for good cause.

The handbook emphasizes:
• Space needs.
• Planning for activities.
• Providing a functional and comfortable living environment.

You will also find help on:
• Social and psychological needs of family members.
• Guidelines on how much you can afford to spend for housing.
• Site and location choices.
• Floor plan evaluation.
• Energy savings.
• Housing choices available, including styles, shapes, types, and construction.

This handbook is only a tool. All households differ; houses take on different characteristics once a family settles in. With careful planning, multiple use rooms, and some compromises, it is usually possible to meet a family's needs and match its lifestyle.

Analyzing Life Style

Where to Begin

• Determine present and future needs based on your family's life cycle stage.
• Determine life style needs and wants of the whole household and of each individual member.
• Determine how much you can afford to spend.
• Expect to make many compromises. No plan is perfect. But the best plan possible can come from time and effort spent on planning.
• Keep notes as you communicate with family members now and with advisers later.

Family Life Cycle Stages

Most households progress through several stages as individuals arrive, mature, and leave. Each change affects the requirements of a home.

Before you start planning or hunting for a house, study the life cycle stages outlined below to determine where you are, and most importantly, where you may be headed relative to a living situation. Try to evaluate your needs for the next one to five or more years. Buying a house more often than once in five years is usually costly.

Single person
• **Life cycle stage.** Usually a person who has left home but is unmarried.
• **Tenure form.** Apartment living is common because mobility is high. Ownership may not be desirable. Housing expenses are more easily controlled.
• **Space needs.** Often one room or a one-bedroom unit, especially in the early years when few furnishings have been acquired.
• **Location.** Locations close to work, recreation, and cultural activities are most important.

Couple
• **Life cycle stage.** During early married years, needs may not change greatly from single persons.
• **Tenure form.** Mobility is still high, so rental may be preferred.
• **Space needs.** Recreation and social contact are important. Living space needs are basic, but may include entertaining, hobbies, or at-home work. More storage is needed for two people and for future purchases.
• **Location.** If both are employed, access to the work of both is important.

Expanding family
• **Life cycle stage.** Time period from the first child's arrival until the last child reaches adolescence.
• **Tenure form.** Owning a single family detached dwelling is usually first choice because it allows adapting, adding, or altering space to meet changing needs. Moving to a larger home is also common.
• **Space needs.** Space needs are approaching the maximum. Especially needed are more bedrooms, baths, and storage, as well as indoor and outdoor play space for children.
• **Location.** Access to shopping, parks, recreation, day care centers, and schools is important.

Launching family
• **Life cycle stage.** Time period when first child reaches adolescence until the last child leaves home.
• **Space needs.** Housing needs are maximum: Extra pressure is on living/recreation areas, because children and adults are involved with friends and business associates. More privacy and a bedroom for parents and for each child are often desired. Children's interests and hobbies add to storage needs. Children tend to leave home with only essentials, leaving other possessions to be stored until later. Flexible space use is needed.
• **Location.** Locations with the best advantages for children are often considered essential.

Empty nest
- **Life cycle stage.** Children have left home, but parents have not retired.
- **Space needs.** Space needs tend to diminish, but pressure on housing may continue: extended visits from children and grandchildren; a child may return, perhaps with a family; space for a parent may be needed. Storage needs remain, because children often store items at home until they get adequate space. And, the couple probably has its maximum level of possessions and needs additional storage.
- **Location.** Couples may want to maintain ties with neighbors and the community rather than move.

Active retirement
- **Life cycle stage.** Retirement has begun, but both spouses (or surviving spouse) are healthy and can live independently.
- **Space needs.** Hobbies and social activities with children or friends are important. Housing costs diminish with a paid-off mortgage. At this stage, a main floor bedroom and bath may become important. Although less space is required, many prefer to remain in their own home. Others move to a setting requiring less upkeep, such as an apartment or condominium. Others convert some unneeded living area into rental space for additional income.

Restricted retirement
- **Life cycle stage.** A health problem with one or both spouses hinders independent living.
- **Tenure form.** At this stage, a move to a smaller home, an apartment, with one of the children, or a facility for the elderly (ranging from independent living units to total-care nursing homes) is often necessary.
- **Space needs.** Living space needed is minimum, but should include space for entertaining friends and relatives. Storage space must be generous for keepsakes. Compact single-story living, privacy, cheerful atmosphere, easy maintenance, safety, and security are special needs. A ground floor (or elevator access) bedroom and bath is needed. Social contact with peers and others is important.
- **Location.** Access to services is important: meals, housekeeping, transportation, medical and social services, etc.

Middle-aged, single adults
- **Life cycle stage.** Some people settle into permanent single-person living; 35 is often considered the crossover age from young single adult to middle-aged status.
- **Tenure form.** Many prefer ownership: condominium, cooperative, or single family detached home.
- **Space needs.** Space needs include a guest bedroom, well equipped kitchen, entertaining space in both the living and dining areas, and storage space for clothes, hobbies, and sports equipment.
- **Location.** Access to recreational facilities, amenities, and work are important.

Single-parent families
- **Life cycle stage.** A single person with children to care for.
- **Tenure form.** Owning a single family detached dwelling is usually sought, because it allows adapting, adding, or altering space to meet changing needs.
- **Space needs.** Needs are similar to those of the two-parent family.
- **Location.** Access to work, shopping, parks, recreation, day care centers, and schools is important.

Unrelated adults
- **Life cycle stage.** Increasingly, unrelated adults are choosing to live together.
- **Tenure form.** Younger adults often rent, because of financial constraints and high mobility; older adults often buy housing.
- **Space needs.** Sharing social and work areas is common. A bedroom may be shared, but needs often include separate private areas for sleeping, study, hobbies, and other recreational activities. Optimally, each has a separate den or study in addition to a bedroom, but a large bedroom can serve.
- **Location.** Convenience to work may be important in the early years, before other interests predominate.

Life Style Needs

Find where you are in the family life cycle to help you think about housing needs. Then consider your life style; focus on how you live, whether you entertain frequently or seldom, or work at home or away. Life style needs help guide you to housing type, layout, shape, and style to meet members' needs and wants adequately, comfortably, and functionally. Assess the living patterns of your household as a group first, and then the patterns of each member.

Living patterns

To determine living patterns, consider the portion of time the family and its members devote to various activities at home. Considering these categories may help:
- Social activities outside the household.
- Family activities.
- Individual activities (study, hobbies, work).
- Private activities (dressing, bathing, personal time).
- Work activities (meals, laundry, cleaning, gardening; school or employment interests).
- Leisure activities (television, computer use, games, music).

Deciding on Your Needs

Individual and family activities and housing needs can be put into a diagram, Fig 1-1, which helps visualize space needs by relating activities. It does not represent a floor plan, but one may grow from it.

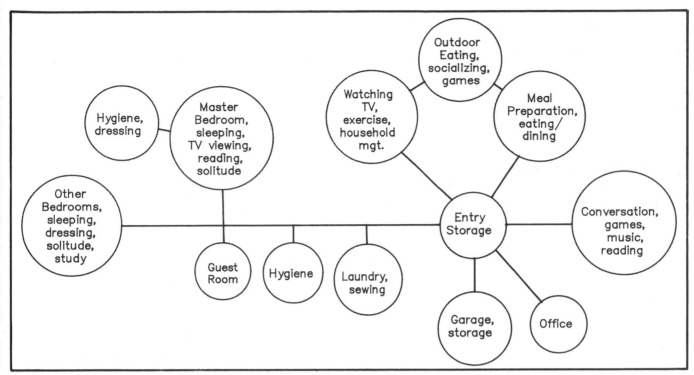

Fig 1-1. Activities inventory bubble diagram.

As you study the bubble diagram, ask each family member what in the present living situation they like and dislike, find the most comfortable, and would like to plan for. For example, a child may want a private room, or an adult may need a place for quiet time each day. Are these needs met with the lists in the diagram?

If there are or will be elderly or physically limited persons in your household, consider their needs now. It is difficult and expensive to change kitchens, baths, halls, doorways, and bedrooms to accommodate their needs later.

Pets play a large role in the lives of many households. Consider their needs, in getting indoors and out, and yours, in caring for them.

Finally, try to picture the future and anticipate activity patterns and needs in five, ten, and twenty years. If the empty nest stage is near, adding space for teenagers to entertain may be justified by other uses for the new space later.

Analyzing Finances

Housing—owned or rented—is often the largest part of household budgets. Purchasing a home could be the largest single investment made in your household's lifetime. Remodeling or renovating an older home is also costly. If you borrow to buy or remodel, the following guidelines may help you determine how much you can afford to spend monthly and still meet other living costs. The guidelines are based on United States household averages.

- Total monthly mortgage payments for principal, interest, real estate taxes, and insurance (PITI): limit to 25%-28% of the borrower's gross monthly income.
- Monthly mortgage payments (PITI) plus monthly installment payments plus other regular monthly debt: limit to 33%-36% of gross monthly income. Installment payments include such items as car or charge card debts that will continue for 10 months. Other regular debt includes alimony or child support.
- Total monthly housing costs: limit to 35%-38% of gross monthly income. Total monthly housing costs are PITI payments plus about 10% for utilities, repairs, and maintenance.

Table 1-1 shows how to apply the guidelines. For example, if household gross monthly income is $1,500, the household may be more comfortable with a monthly mortgage payment (PITI) below $420 ($1,500 × .28). Limit total monthly housing costs in the new dwelling to $570.00 (1,500 × .38). Finally, total monthly income committed to PITI and installment debt should not exceed $540.00 ($1,500 × .36).

To apply the guidelines to your situation, fill in the blanks in Table 1-1. Then visit with lending sources to see if their lending criteria agree.

Table 1-1. Guidelines: How much you can afford for housing.
Items A, B, and C give three different measures of reasonable debt limits. Calculate and compare the results from A, B, and C. Reduce your budget for mortgage, or modify other living expenses if your costs are above the guidelines.

	Example	Your case
Annual income	$18,000.00	$ _____
Monthly income (Annual income ÷ 12)	$ 1,500.00	$ _____
A. Principal, interest, real estate taxes, and insurance (PITI): 25%-28% of gross monthly income: ($1,500 × .28)	$ 420.00	$ _____
B. PITI plus utilities, repairs, and maintenance: about 35% to 38% of gross monthly income: ($1,500 × .38)	$ 570.00	$ _____
C. PITI plus installment and regular debt: about 33% to 36% of gross monthly income: ($1,500 × .36)	$ 540.00	$ _____

Compare with your regular debts + PITI:

	Example	Your case
Car	$100.00	$ _____
Charge cards	$ 20.00	$ _____
Store charge	$ _____	$ _____
Other, list:	$ _____	$ _____
_____	$ _____	$ _____
_____	$ _____	$ _____
Total	$120.00	$ _____
+ PITI (See above)	$420.00 = $540	$ _____ = $ _____

2. LOCATION, SITE, AND APPROACH

When you build or buy, location and site are important. Some of the choices are:

- Areas zoned for multiunit housing such as apartment houses and condominiums.
- Platted housing developments specifying house location by set back and side yard requirements.
- Rural non-farm locations, which allow more freedom in house placement, orientation, and plan selection, but which may also require considering water supply, waste disposal, and areas around the property.
- On-farm locations, which must include relating the house to the farming enterprise and farmstead facilities.

The Neighborhood

Neighborhood character is important. Buy or build in a well maintained or improving neighborhood, not a deteriorating one. The average value of houses in the neighborhood greatly affects the value of your house, and one of well above-average value may sell for less than its real value. A well maintained house in a good quality neighborhood has greater resale value.

Consider the items listed below. Select the ones important to you. If the neighborhood lacks them, you may want to look elsewhere.

Neighbors. Are neighbors compatible with your lifestyle? Will some be in your age and interest group? Are their children in the same age group as yours? Will they help watch your house when you are away?

Schools. Proximity is important, but children grow up and needs change. Busing may make a site farther out suitable.

Shopping. Being close to a shopping area may be important depending on how often you shop.

Place of worship. Proximity to your church may be very important to you depending on your activities and available transportation.

Parks. With a park in walking distance, you can take advantage of facilities you help pay for. A busy playground next door or across the street could detract from the livability of your property.

Recreation. Are nearby recreational facilities of interest? Will they add to or detract from the neighborhood? For example, golf courses are quiet, beautiful, and usually have limited traffic. But, race tracks can be noisy, dusty, and create heavy traffic. Consider how various facilities appeal to your family and how they will affect property values.

Transportation and traffic. It is nice to get to and from work easily and quickly. Is public transportation available, well established, and likely to continue?

Living near a traffic artery is convenient, but you may want to avoid noise and exhaust fumes. Consider possible changing traffic patterns: undeveloped areas can cause congested roads later; traffic past the house can be too great a hazard, or the road may be widened or relocated. Is maintenance, including snow removal, reasonable?

Water. Surface water during heavy rainfall or snow melt could be a problem. Does the area around you drain across your site or away from it? Is subsurface drainage adequate? Nearby creeks or rivers may be an attraction, but they can also flood or be a hazard to young children. Lakes may be attractive but can add to insect populations and could become polluted. Check with local and state health authorities about ground water pollution.

Sewage disposal and landfill facilities. Even under the best management, odors, mosquitoes and rodents are of concern. Distance is the best assurance that quality of living will not be affected.

Noise, odor, pollutants. Locate the sources you want to avoid. Evaluate seasonal prevailing wind directions. Do not buy property downwind from a source unless enough distance dilutes its effects. Heavy traffic and occasional high noise levels affect sites near airports.

Hospital and health care. Families need both. Long distances and inconvenient travel can add risks, costs, and anxieties for those using health care services.

Police and fire protection. Availability is of concern to many. Police protection is needed more in some neighborhoods than others. Fire hydrants are often not available in rural areas. Fire department and hydrant locations can affect fire insurance rates.

Your Building Site

Consider the following relative to your lot:

Legal. Check the title, deed, and zoning restrictions. An attorney may be needed to interpret restrictions, liens and use limitations.

Zoning. Is your lot and the area around you zoned to suit your needs? Is it single or multiple family? Are fences permitted? Are zoning regulations changing or have they been stable for some time? Changes could help or hurt you.

City growth patterns. Property values in the path of a city's expansion may rise. But if the city is growing away from you, your neighborhood may deteriorate, causing properties to lose value.

Future development. Changes close to your site may increase or decrease property values. If possible, check with local planning officials for clues to future developments and their effect on your property.

Building codes. What building codes apply? How long have they been in effect? Building codes properly applied are meant to assure quality and safety in house construction.

Orientation. Can you develop a plan with the desired orientation on the lot you are considering? Desirable features often include orientation with respect to sun, wind, outdoor living, and views. What the neighbors have done can affect developing your lot.

Sun access. Utilizing active and passive solar systems is common today. Be sure you have continued sun access. Trees—yours or your neighbors—may block the sun as they grow.

Soil characteristics. Is the soil well drained, both surface and subsurface? Check with present residents and local housing inspection officials. Ask about backups from storm and sanitary sewers, local practices for sump pumps, and whether neighbors use their basements for living space. Are wet basements a problem? Will the soil support a garden and vigorous lawn growth? Beware of a lot containing fill soil—it may settle. Avoid conditions that can hold or carry water near the surface during the wet season. Is the soil in a chemical waste hazard area?

Utilities. Your lot should have access to water, gas, electricity, telephone, sewers, and street lights. If they are not available, what will they cost? Aerial lines for power and phone service are common, but underground lines are preferred. Check the location and depth of sanitary and storm sewers. If less than 6' deep, you may have trouble with basement drainage. If a private sewage system is needed, will zoning, space, and soil type permit a septic tank or will a more expensive system be required? The time to discuss these items is before you buy the lot.

Sidewalks, curbs, and pavement. Are these in and paid for? If not, does each owner pay for pavings in front of his lot or does city, county or state pay for improvements?

Lot size and shape. Narrow lots are hard to work with—the length of the house is usually perpendicular to the street. An attached garage may not be possible. A lot at least 60' wide may be more expensive but worth the difference. Wedge-shaped lots require careful house design to avoid an awkward arrangement. Is there enough space for an addition; are they permitted? Is there enough outdoor recreation space?

Immediate surroundings. Is the neighborhood attractive and well maintained? Variation of site plans and house styles should be consistent with the size and value of your proposed house. Among large houses, the value of your small one may be enhanced. If you have the one large house, the reverse may be true.

Special Considerations for Rural Sites

Choosing a rural or farm site is similar to selecting an urban site. Review the above factors. If the farmstead is already located, the problem may be to fit the house into a rather limited area. Consider locating away from the farmstead. Location of a farm house is unique—it is part of a total farm business. Fig 2-1 is an example of a well planned farmstead.

A rural non-farm site may offer more freedom of location. Be aware of activities on surrounding property. Some rural enterprises make objectionable neighbors. Agricultural lands usually make good neighbors, but not always. Odors and flies from livestock can be annoying. Odors from manure spread on nearby fields can be objectionable.

The following points help select a suitable rural site.

Approach to house. The house should be the first major building reached when entering a farmstead from public roads. Provide obvious guest parking for 3 to 6 cars and turn-around space. Avoid dangerous backing onto a public road when possible. Design walks and landscaping to lead visitors to the guest entry. Avoid planting shrubs, trees, and crops that obstruct vision at the road.

Distance from main road. Put the house at least 100' from the road if possible, to allow for road widening and to buffer noise and dust. Too much distance adds to driveway maintenance.

Space available for house and yard. Do not crowd a large house into a small space. Leave room to accentuate the building with plantings. Consider possible irrigation patterns. A larger yard means more maintenance, but the results can be rewarding.

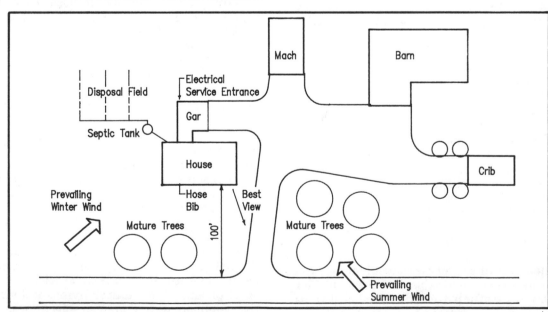

Fig 2-1. House location in a farmstead.

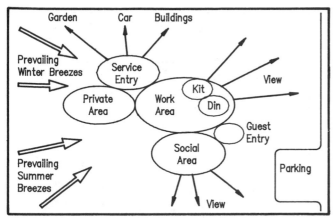

Fig 2-2. House zones relative to exterior factors.

Drainage. Drain the farmyard and livestock areas away from the house. Intercept and divert surface water far enough from the house to allow an adequate, well drained yard. Avoid a site where underground flow or a high water table can interfere with basements, footings, and foundations. Soil from excavating a basement can often build the final grade to provide drainage.

View. Take advantage of pleasant countryside views. In general, provide a view from the kitchen or service area toward the farm courtyard and service buildings and, if practical, the drive and public road. These views help detect accidents, fire, loose livestock, or anyone coming or going from the farmstead.

Windbreaks and trees. Tree windbreaks are usually desirable if healthy and properly located. They can improve comfort, but they may block a desirable view or the sun, and a snowdrift along a windbreak can be 75'-100' wide. Contact your county Cooperative Extension agent for detailed planning resources.

If there is a choice of good locations, favor the one with trees to get a head start in landscaping and shade. However, if their variety is undesirable or their location interferes with house orientation or sun utilization, select another site.

Wind. Try to orient doors, windows, and outdoor living areas to use cooling summer breezes. Protect house entries from cold wind and snow with careful design of a new or remodeled house, as with an airlock, Fig 5-2.

Odors. Locate the house upwind (southwest in most midwest areas) from livestock facilities to minimize odors carried by prevailing summer winds. Keep the house at least 200' from a livestock operation. Consider locating the house away from the present farmstead.

Dimensions for Site Planning

Walkways, Steps, and Stoops

Make the approach to a house inviting and safe. The guest entry walkway should accommodate two people side by side and the steps should be comfortable. The stoop at the door should be large enough for people with canes, crutches, or wheelchairs and to allow a screen or storm door to open out. See Table 2-1 and Fig 2-3.

Table 2-1. Walkway dimensions.

	Recommended	Minimum
Walkway to guest entry	5' wide	4' wide
Other walkways	2½' wide	2' wide
Stoop (platform at doorway)	5'x5'	4'x4'
Steps		6" rise, 12" tread

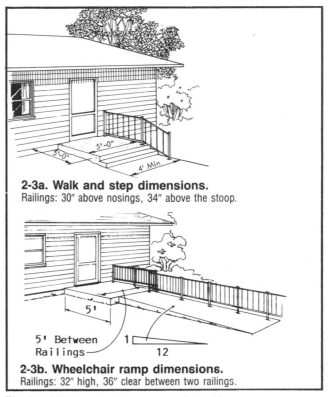

2-3a. Walk and step dimensions.
Railings: 30" above nosings, 34" above the stoop.

2-3b. Wheelchair ramp dimensions.
Railings: 32" high, 36" clear between two railings.

Fig 2-3. Walk, step, and ramp dimensions.
A railing is recommended for both sides. It is shown here on only one side for clarity of dimensions. See the handicapped discussion in Chapter 5.

Driveways and Parking

The dimensions in Figs 2-4 through 2-6 provide space to walk past a parked car without stepping off the driveway into wet grass or snow. Increase the 12' width of a single drive to 18' for a double drive. The 30' outside radius (12' drive + 18' radius) can be 28' if the front of the car can extend beyond the drive.

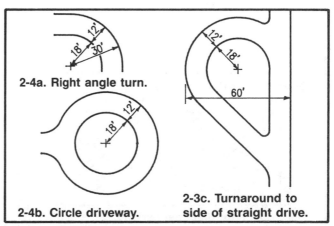

2-4a. Right angle turn.

2-4b. Circle driveway.

2-3c. Turnaround to side of straight drive.

Fig 2-4. Driveway turns.
Cars and pickup trucks.

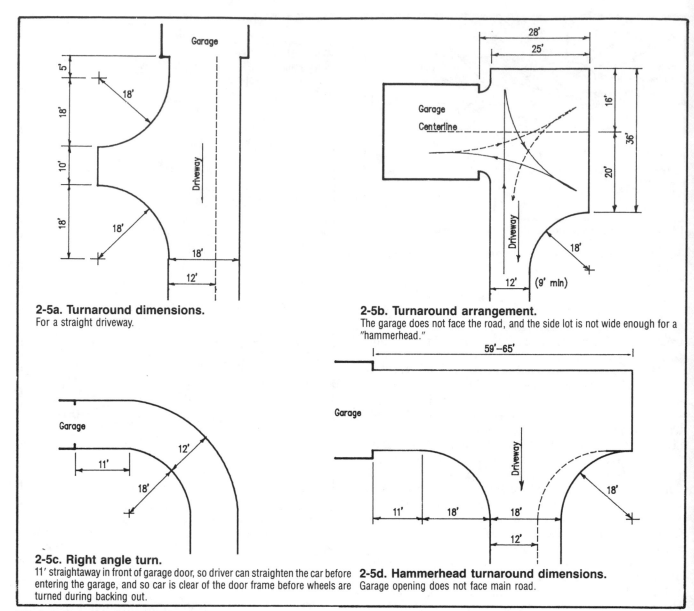

2-5a. Turnaround dimensions.
For a straight driveway.

2-5b. Turnaround arrangement.
The garage does not face the road, and the side lot is not wide enough for a "hammerhead."

2-5c. Right angle turn.
11' straightaway in front of garage door, so driver can straighten the car before entering the garage, and so car is clear of the door frame before wheels are turned during backing out.

2-5d. Hammerhead turnaround dimensions.
Garage opening does not face main road.

Fig 2-5. Garage approaches.

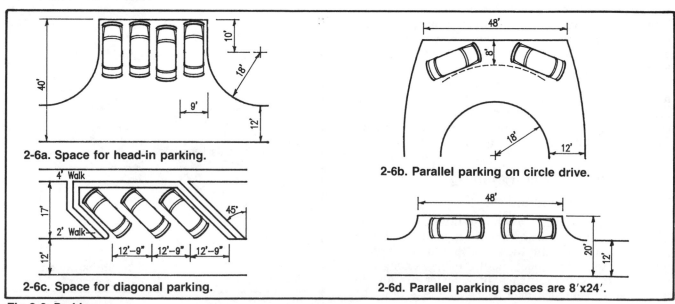

2-6a. Space for head-in parking.

2-6b. Parallel parking on circle drive.

2-6c. Space for diagonal parking.

2-6d. Parallel parking spaces are 8'x24'.

Fig 2-6. Parking.
Off-street guest parking on urban lot or parking near guest entry of a farm house.

3. EVALUATING FLOOR PLANS

The floor plan of a house largely determines its convenience, livability and satisfaction.

Look for plans with flexible space, good traffic patterns, and maximum storage potential. Whether you are building a new home, considering an existing home or apartment, or remodeling your present home, thoroughly evaluate the floor plan. Consider:
- Activity areas (how the house is zoned for work, social, and private activities).
- Traffic patterns (how you move from room to room and through rooms).
- Room relationships (how one room functions relative to others).
- Details of individual rooms and other spaces. Note the amount of storage space throughout the plan.

Abbreviations for room names are in Table 3-1.

Table 3-1. Room abbreviations.

Abbr	
B	Bath
BR	Bedroom
CL	Closet/Storage
DA	Dining Area
DR	Dining Room
FR	Family Room
G	Garage
K	Kitchen
LR	Living Room
OFF	Office
SD	Sliding Door
U	Utility

Activity Zones

A floor plan is usually more workable and satisfying if activities are separated into zones. Zoning relates activity areas that need to relate (such as kitchen and dining) and separates those that interfere with each other (noisy vs. quiet activities).

The three areas to consider are **work, social,** and **private.** As you study house plans, look for the three areas to be well defined and reasonably separated, as in Fig 3-1. An area may be divided; bedrooms or living and recreation rooms can be on more than one floor or in separate areas of a single floor.

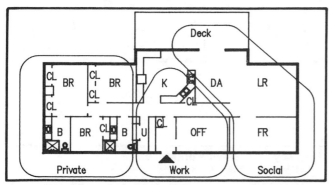

Fig 3-1. House zoned for desired room relationships.
Plan developed from bubble diagram, Chapter 1.

Work Areas

The primary work areas are the kitchen, laundry, utility, and office areas. They can be together in one work area or separated. With two or three work areas in a house, allow for moving easily from one to another with minimum steps or disturbance of other family activities. Plan each part of a work area to be complete and efficient.

Social Areas

The social area can be one specific area such as living room, dining area, patio, and guest entry. Or there can be two or more social areas such as living and family rooms separated by a kitchen, and a study or library in another part of the house. An informal social area can be combined with the kitchen. Match the number and size of social areas to the family's needs and resources.

Private Areas

Grouping bedrooms and baths in one area separates them from the social and work areas. Some plans separate the master bedroom and bath from the others. With the private area on the second floor, a half bath and temporary sleeping space on the main floor allows for the sick or handicapped. See Service Entry, Chapter 5.

Fig 3-1 is an example of a well zoned house.

Traffic Patterns

When you first step into a house or look at a floor plan, visualize traffic moving through the house. The best traffic patterns allow access from the entries to all activity areas without using any room as a corridor. If the traffic pattern is poor, look for another plan rather than wasting time evaluating individual rooms.

Traffic flow should not interfere with a good furniture arrangement or activities within a room. Traffic must not interfere with private areas. A central hall helps control traffic. Fig 3-2 illustrates traffic patterns.

Consider traffic between levels in a multilevel house. Locate stairways for convenience. For example, if recreation and entertainment space are in the basement, the basement stairs may start down from the central hall, Fig 3-3. But if the basement has only the heating system and storage of seldom-used items, stair location is less important, Fig 3-4.

When the second floor in a two-story house is primarily for sleeping, locate stairs for bedroom access without crossing other rooms. Put the stairs to the second floor above the basement stairs for efficient space use. A hallway location of the stairs is desirable. Consider space use at each level when locating the stairs, Fig 3-5.

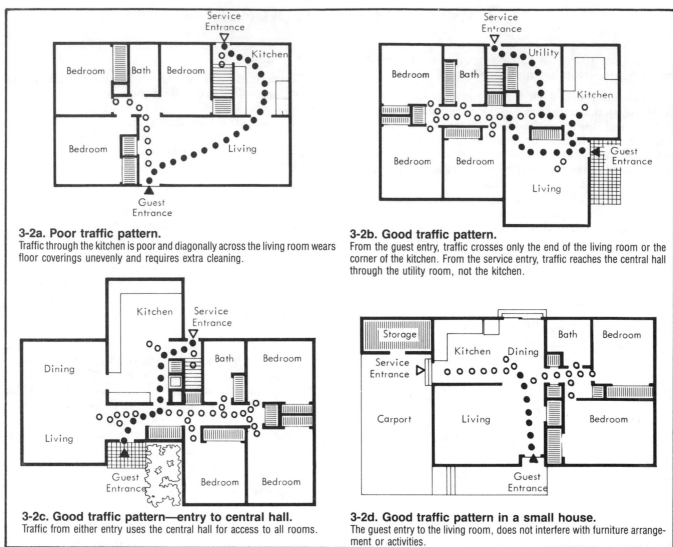

3-2a. Poor traffic pattern.
Traffic through the kitchen is poor and diagonally across the living room wears floor coverings unevenly and requires extra cleaning.

3-2b. Good traffic pattern.
From the guest entry, traffic crosses only the end of the living room or the corner of the kitchen. From the service entry, traffic reaches the central hall through the utility room, not the kitchen.

3-2c. Good traffic pattern—entry to central hall.
Traffic from either entry uses the central hall for access to all rooms.

3-2d. Good traffic pattern in a small house.
The guest entry to the living room, does not interfere with furniture arrangement or activities.

Fig 3-2. Traffic patterns.

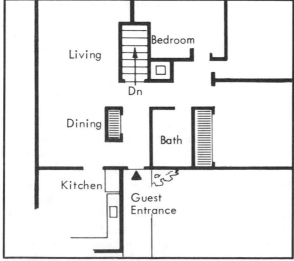

Fig 3-3. Stairway from central hall.
Central stairway to lower level social area.

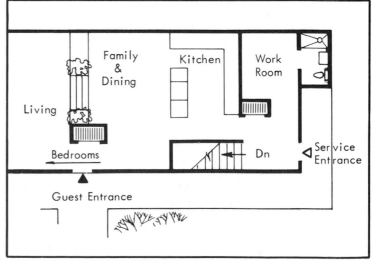

Fig 3-4. Stairway near service entrance.
Stairway for access to lower level utilities.

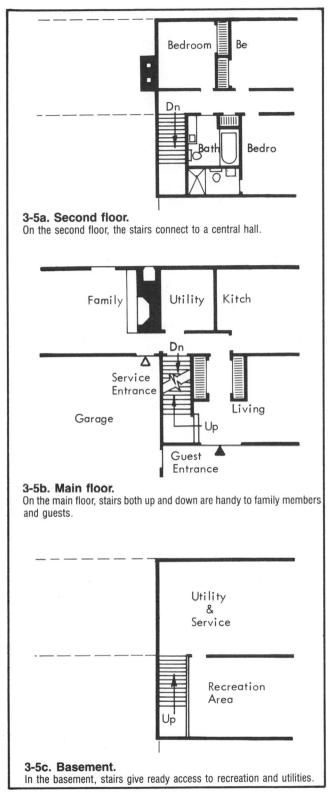

3-5a. Second floor.
On the second floor, the stairs connect to a central hall.

3-5b. Main floor.
On the main floor, stairs both up and down are handy to family members and guests.

3-5c. Basement.
In the basement, stairs give ready access to recreation and utilities.

Fig 3-5. Good stairway system in a two-story house.

Room or Space Relationships

The relationship of one room to another influences the way the floor plan functions. Some examples of room relationships to consider:

- The kitchen near the family eating area takes priority over other dining areas where an occasional meal is served.

- If food is frequently prepared or served on a patio, its relationship to the kitchen is important. Avoid carrying food through the garage to a patio.
- Make the more formal dining area adjacent to the living area and accessible from the kitchen.
- If there is only one bathroom, it should be accessible without going through another room.
- With more than one bathroom, make one easily accessible from social and work areas as well as from the private area, while another may be reserved for the master bedroom. Both sight and sound privacy are important.
- A sewing center might be near the kitchen, so meal preparation and sewing can dovetail, or near family evening activities.

Consider how interior and exterior spaces relate, Fig 3-6:

- Put a patio or deck near the kitchen, social area, or master bedroom.
- Locate a children's play yard where it can be seen from inside the house, preferably from the kitchen.
- Gardening relates to utility area or kitchen.
- Clotheslines serve the laundry room.
- An attached sunspace relates to social area and kitchen, preferably on the south side of house.

Open Floor Plans

Except for bedrooms and bathrooms, spaces in a house need not be divided with walls, Fig 3-6. For example, meal preparation, dining, and relaxation may all be in one open space. In an **open plan,** divide activity areas, not with walls, but with dividers, furniture, screens, planters, or sliding or folding doors.

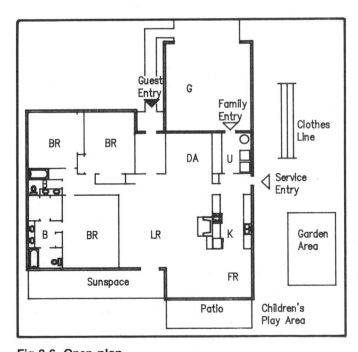

Fig 3-6. Open plan.
Note how interior and exterior spaces relate.

Open plans are flexible and can be changed for different events or changing family life styles.

Consider these features of open floor plans:

- Smaller houses seem larger if spaces are visually connected.
- Heating and cooling are more efficient.
- Open plans accommodate larger groups in a smaller home and allow more flexible room arrangements.
- Clutter is visible.
- Sounds transfer easily.
- Reduced wall space may affect placing furniture with unfinished backs.
- Half walls can divide space without blocking views.
- Floor surfaces can help show areas and uses—carpet for furniture groupings and hard surface for traffic.
- Floor levels and ceiling heights can separate areas, but a change in floor level can restrict the space use.
- Moveable dividers (screens, fabric hangings) can divide areas and are temporary and flexible.
- Private areas are more functional when separated from work and social areas of an open plan.
- Open plans need effective, convenient storage and furniture serving more than one function.
- The long spans over open areas may create framing problems that are easily overcome with roof trusses in one-story houses and floor trusses in two-story construction.

4. HOUSING SHAPES AND TYPES

Knowing about different housing shapes and types allows visualizing a number of ways the bubble diagram and floor plan can be arranged.

Shapes of Living Units

Zoning, good traffic flow, and thoughtful room relationships are available in houses of many different shapes. Living units are square, circular, atrium or court, rectangular, and letter shape. Each shape has advantages or disadvantages, depending on how well the designer has applied good planning principles. Each basic shape can be one story, 1½ story, split level, or multi-story. Abbreviations for room names are in Table 3-1. Appliance symbols are in Fig 9-4.

Circular Plan

Advantages
- Least perimeter (length of exterior walls) of any shape for floor area enclosed.
- Can blend well into the natural landscape.
- Cast-in-place concrete and urethane foam adapt well for construction.

Disadvantages
- More expensive to build because of unique construction.
- Requires site that lets it blend with adjoining houses.
- May be less attractive to buyers or financiers.
- Uses non-rectangular floor coverings.

Square Plan

Advantages
- Usually less expensive to build than a rectangle because of less perimeter for a given floor area, although roof framing could be relatively expensive.
- Can be built on a smaller lot.
- Produces a compact design.
- Less hallway area—rooms are easily reached from any part of the house.

Disadvantages
- House zones cannot be as well defined as in rectangular plans.
- Box-like appearance.
- Less flexible for adding on.

Atrium or Court Plan

An atrium is an open and usually unroofed area near the center of the plan. It may be enclosed with a skylight. The layout is an enlarged version of square, circular, or rectangular plans. Variations are often used in an underground house.

Advantages
- More possibilities for separating activity areas.
- Very private outdoor (atrium) area.
- More natural lighting.

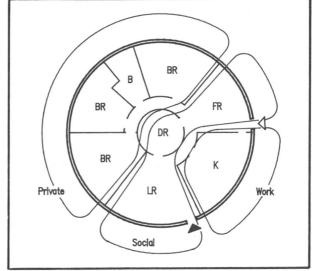

Fig 4-1. Circular plan.

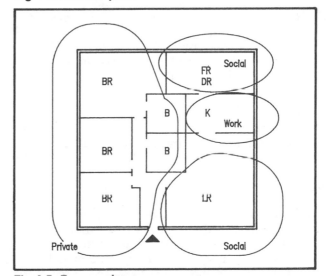

Fig 4-2. Square plan.

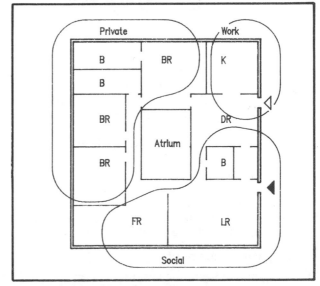

Fig 4-3. Atrium or court plan.

Disadvantages
- More expensive, because it requires more foundation, wall area, and land.
- More exposed wall area around open atriums increase utility costs.

Rectangular Plan
Advantages
- House zones can be well defined with more possibilities in locating activity areas.
- Uses conventional building materials better than round or irregular shapes.

Disadvantage
- Requires more hallway space to provide easy access to all areas.

Letter Shape Plans

L, U, T, E, and H shapes often appear in floor plans.

Advantages
- Shape is good for zoning activities.
- Good for separating parent private areas from other private areas.
- Can create sheltered outdoor area.
- Outside areas can easily expand social areas and relate to indoor activities.

Disadvantages
- More expensive.
- Requires more foundation, wall area, and land.
- Plumbing and heating costs are higher.
- Roof is usually more complicated.

Multilevel Plans

All floor plan shapes can be multilevel. With the same foundation and roof, and by adding partial or full stories, multilevel plans provide living space at a minimum cost per square foot. Options include one story with full basement; 1½, two, and three story with or without basement; split level; and raised ranch. Each type has features that are advantages or disadvantages.

Basement
- Space at relatively low cost for utilities (heating plant, water heater, etc.), storage, workshop, hobby areas, and recreation. Can be finished for bedrooms if windows or door provide adequate emergency exit.
- Provides separation for noisy or dirty operations from social areas.
- Storm shelter.
- To make efficient use of space, provide good access and window area.
- Can be difficult to keep dry.
- Can be difficult to ventilate.

One Story with Basement
- Very popular style for resale.
- Major living areas on one level.

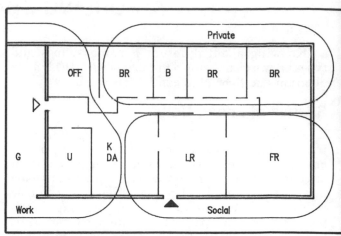

Fig 4-4. Rectangular plan.

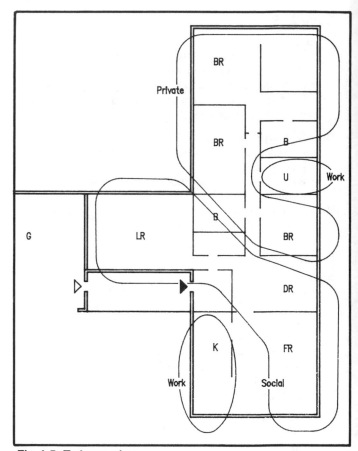

Fig 4-5. T-shape plan.

- Less stairway climbing than other multilevel styles.
- Does not provide as much separation between private and social areas as other multilevel styles.

Split Level or Trilevel
- Lower level partly above ground has better light and ventilation than basements. It may allow a walk-out basement. A typical basement is often included under the ground floor level.
- Upper level for bedrooms and baths separates private and social areas better than many one story plans.

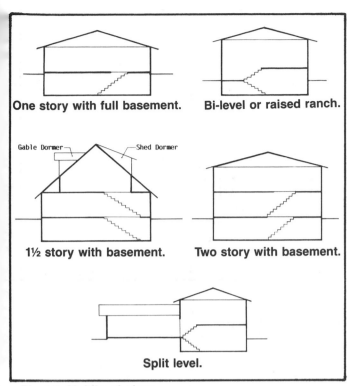

One story with full basement.   Bi-level or raised ranch.

Gable Dormer —   — Shed Dormer

1½ story with basement.   Two story with basement.

Split level.

Fig 4-6. Multilevel plans.

- Half flights of stairs are easier to negotiate than full flights.
- Stairways are used many times a day, which is especially undesirable for elderly or handicapped.
- Uniform heating and cooling at all three levels requires careful design.
- May suit a sloping lot.

1½ Story

- Minimum roof and foundation for space enclosed.
- Expandable space—second floor can be finished when needed.
- With one bedroom and bath on the first floor, it effectively converts to a one bedroom house by closing off the second floor.
- Steep roof is needed to provide headroom upstairs.

Two Story

- Maximum above-ground living area for dollar invested.
- Especially desirable for large families needing more bedroom-bathroom area.
- A first floor bath and a sleeping room for ill or aged are recommended.
- May have more space on second floor than needed if second floor is same size as first floor.

Bi-level or Raised Ranch

- Fewer moisture problems and more adequate windows in lower level than in a basement. Building codes may require large windows if bedrooms are in a basement.
- Lower level may be better living space than a basement.

- Must always go up or down a half flight of stairs from the guest entry, and a half or full flight from the service entry.
- Not suited to elderly or handicapped.
- Needs to relate to site to be esthetically pleasing.

Types of Living Units

Both single family and multifamily units can satisfy housing needs. Multi-family units are duplex, 3- or 4-plex, town or row house (cluster), mid-to-high-rise, and garden or penthouse apartments.

Single Family Unit

The single family unit is the traditional house meeting the needs of one family. Expandable or dividable housing, or tandem living units, may become important as the family changes.

Tandem Living

Individuals or couples may be able to afford better housing with greater security in tandem (together) than alone. Tandem units can be designed with well separated private areas for each person or couple, and central living, kitchen, and utility areas to be shared. Tandem units are in both single-unit and multiunit housing. See Fig 4-7.

Multiunits

Multiunit housing is common during several life cycle stages. Evaluate multiunit housing the same way as single units; the space and other planning principles are the same.

Multiunits are popular in small towns as well as cities. Costs tend to be lower, because of more housing units per acre than with single units. This type of housing is often closer to work or town centers. Good planning can provide privacy for each unit. Outdoor maintenance may be provided by the housing owners, either in rentals or by a neighbor-association fee in owned housing units.

The "plex" units and town or row houses usually provide an outdoor area with each unit, such as a deck or patio. Fig 4-8. Driveways and walks may be shared. Good planning and construction can reduce noise between living units and patios or decks. Check for soundproofing in adjoining walls and screening and spacing between outdoor living areas.

Town and row houses have three or more units in a row. Units adjoin with no space between, Fig 4-9. Shared walls and reduced heating and land costs reduce unit costs; privacy and some outdoor living area are still provided. Noise can be a disadvantage. Be sure units are separated by adequate firewalls.

Apartments are often divided into type by the number of stories—garden (low-rise), mid-rise, and high-rise. Be sure there is a fire exit from each story.

- Garden apartment: one or two stories with outdoor garden or ground area with each unit.
- Low-rise: two to three stories (called "walk-ups"). They are unsuitable for handicapped or aged persons.
- Mid-rise: four to five stories in the structure; usually has an elevator.
- High-rise: six or more stories high with elevator.

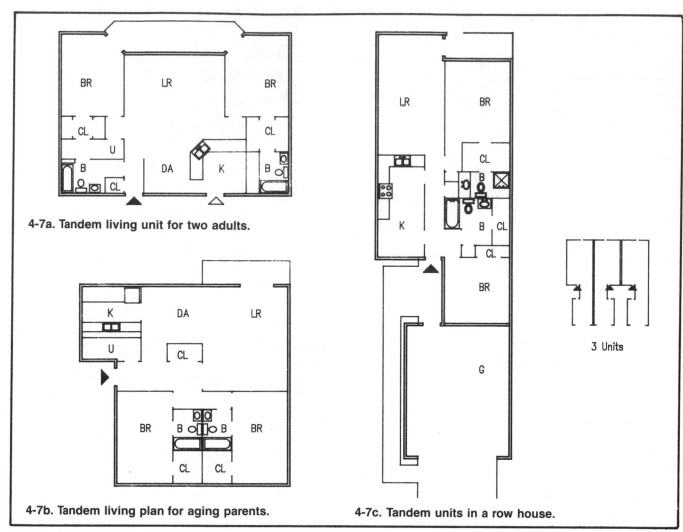

4-7a. Tandem living unit for two adults.

4-7b. Tandem living plan for aging parents.

4-7c. Tandem units in a row house.

Fig 4-7. Tandem units.

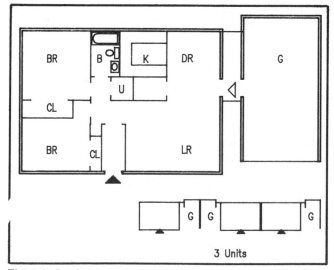

Fig 4-8. Duplex.

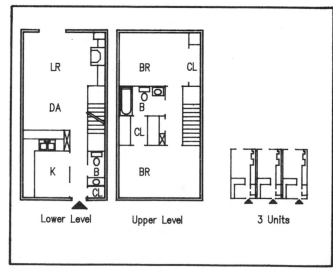

Fig 4-9. Townhouse.

5. ENTRIES, HALLS, STAIRS, AND DOORS

The dimensions of the paths into and through a house are as important as room dimensions. Traffic patterns are discussed in Chapter 3. Adapting for wheelchair access is discussed at the end of this chapter.

Entries

Entries control circulation throughout the house. Family members or guests should be able to reach other areas of the house without interfering with activities in any room.

"Guest" and "service" are terms used in this book to describe the two main entries of a house; entries are not necessarily on the front and back.

Guest Entry

If this entry is near the center of the house rather than at one end, a better indoor traffic pattern is usually possible. Fig 5-1 shows access to zones in the house from a well located guest entry.

Relocating an entry in an existing house is one way to improve traffic flow and space use. First lay out the activity areas and determine where the entry best relates to these areas. Put the entry where there is the most traffic. Access to the social and work areas is more important than to the private area.

Once the general location is established, consider the room into which it opens. Furniture arrangement is more flexible with the entry at the end, rather than the center, of a room.

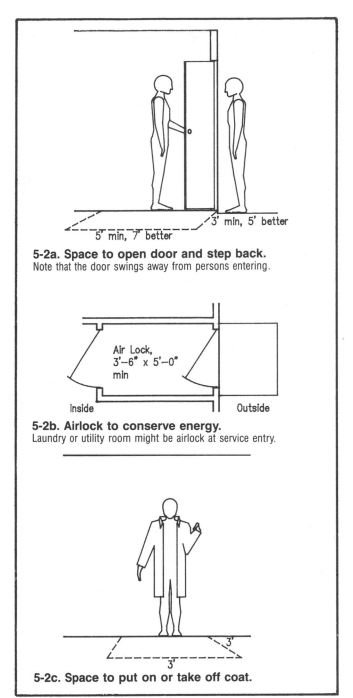

5-2a. Space to open door and step back.
Note that the door swings away from persons entering.

5-2b. Airlock to conserve energy.
Laundry or utility room might be airlock at service entry.

5-2c. Space to put on or take off coat.

Fig 5-2. Space at guest entry.

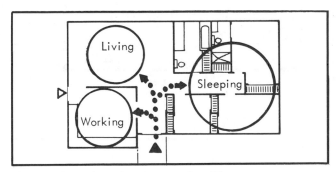

Fig 5-1. Entry location for good traffic pattern.
For energy conservation, consider an airlock at guest and service entries.

Space requirements

Space at an entry varies with the size of the house, activities, and how many people use the area. Swing the door away from persons entering. Avoid having to walk around a door to enter a room.

Storage at guest entry

Provide a closet for guests' and family members' outdoor clothing. Fig 5-3 is an example. A closet just beyond the door is handier than one behind the door, Fig 5-4.

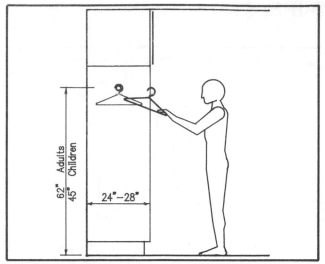

Fig 5-3. Entry storage.
Rod height and clear closet depth for coats on hangers. With hooks instead of hangers, a closet need be only 12″-16″ deep. Put hooks about 62″ high for adults and 45″ for children or wheelchair users.

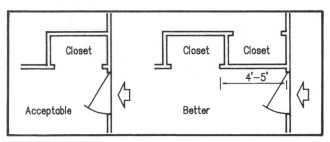

Fig 5-4. Avoid closets behind doors.

Service Entry

Access to work areas is most important in planning the service entry. Most supplies coming in are for the food preparation area. Family members may want to wash before a meal. Laundry may be taken in and out of this entry. Provide access to social or private areas without interfering with work area activities.

Especially in farm houses, provide space to remove and store work clothing and boots, as well as cleanup facilities. Children coming in from play may also use these facilities. A walk-in shower may be preferred to a tub. If a complete bath is not possible, a lavatory and toilet are highly recommended.

Fig 5-5 shows some possible arrangements at the service entry. A rack with a drip pan below may be provided for shoes and boots. Make sure air can circulate to dry damp coats and shoes. A chair or bench is convenient for putting on shoes or boots and for assisting a child.

Halls

Widths of hallways connecting a series of rooms are in Table 5-1. Consider making longer halls wider. Think ahead to moving furniture in and out. Wheelchair or walker access may someday be needed. Wider halls permit pictures or other wall decorations.

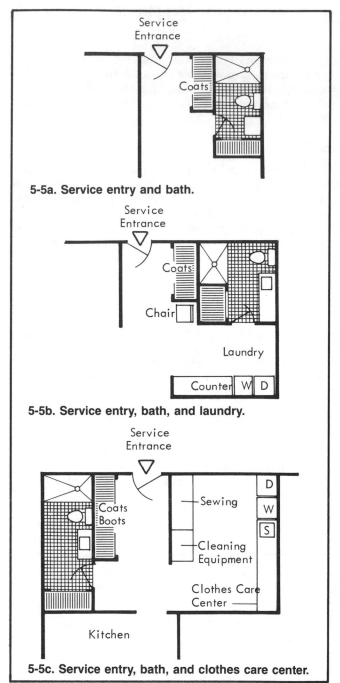

5-5a. Service entry and bath.

5-5b. Service entry, bath, and laundry.

5-5c. Service entry, bath, and clothes care center.

Fig 5-5. Service entries.
See chapters on planning bathrooms and clothes care centers.

Table 5-1. Hall widths.

Hall width	Comments
36″	Minimum
40″	Recommended for most halls
42″	Halls 16′-24′ long and for wheelchair users
48″ or more	Halls 24′ or longer and commercial buildings

Interior Stairs

Stairs provide access from one level to another. Young children, older adults, and the physically handicapped find stairs difficult. Allow enough room

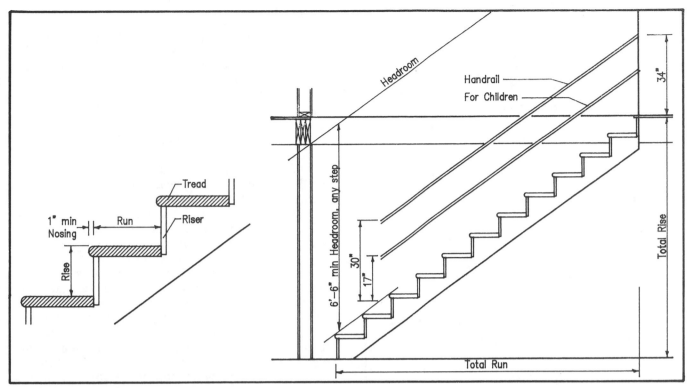

Fig 5-6. Stair dimensions.

to make stairs easy to use. Light them well. Plan door swings carefully to minimize hazards.

Stairs can lead straight from one area to another, or they can turn. Straight stairs with straight entries and exits are easiest to climb, especially if you are carrying something that hides the steps. It is much easier to move furniture on straight stairs. A landing, even in a straight stair, is a convenient resting spot and reduces the distance to fall if you should trip.

Often, a straight stair is not possible. Stairs can turn 90° (a right angle turn) or 180° (a U-turn) at a landing. The service entry is sometimes below the main floor level, with two or three steps up to the kitchen or utility area were typical. The landing and a right angle turn, Fig 5-7a., are inconvenient. If possible, raise the service entry to avoid the landing in a new house. Landscape and grade outdoors to a gradual sloped entry without steps. See Fig 5-6 for recommended stair dimensions.

Two undesirable turns are shown in Fig 5-7. Avoid tapered treads: only part of the tread is wide enough for comfort and safety. Circular stairs have been called space savers. But, for a 34″ wide tread, the opening must be 7′x7′, which saves little space. A second set of stairs is needed to move furniture.

Cantilevered, open, and hanging stairs can enhance an open floor plan. New materials and techniques have made exciting designs possible. Remember that some people may feel uncomfortable on open stairs.

For infrequent access to an attic space, consider a disappearing stair which folds up into the ceiling when not in use.

Space requirements

Total floor space required depends on tread width, riser height, stair opening width, headroom, and

stair type. Safe and comfortable stairs match the stride of an average person stepping up (riser height) and forward (tread depth). If rise increases, decrease tread to avoid tripping over the nosing. See Fig 5-6 and Table 5-2.

Recommended run is about 10″. Avoid runs of less than 9″ or more than 12″. Note: tread = run + nosing. The average rise is 7¼″. Avoid rises of less than 6½″ or more than 8″. Runs and rises outside the recommended ranges are prohibited by many building codes.

Smaller risers are easier to climb but require more floor space and larger floor openings to maintain headroom. Table 5-2 shows the effect of the number and size of risers on the size of the floor opening.

One formula for a safe rise-run ratio is: Rise plus run equals 17 to 17½. A second is: Rise times run equals 73 to 78. A third is: 2 risers plus 1 tread equals 24 to 25. Ask local building officials if there are code requirements in your community.

Uniform steps reduce tripping and stumbling. Make each tread, each riser, and each nosing (including landings) the same dimension. Locate railings as shown in Fig 5-6.

The minimum stair width is 36″ (34″ min. clear tread); wider widths are also used. Although stairs take a lot of room, **generous stair dimensions work better than minimums.**

During house planning, allow about 12′ long and 4′ wide for a floor opening, plus a landing if needed. Determine the actual opening after setting ceiling heights. Set actual dimensions for run and rise after the house is partly built and after measuring exact story height and floor thickness.

Storage can be built over the end of the stair, but maintain headroom clearance.

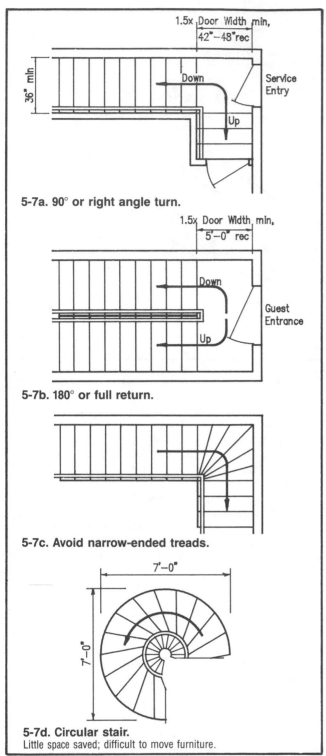

5-7a. 90° or right angle turn.

5-7b. 180° or full return.

5-7c. Avoid narrow-ended treads.

5-7d. Circular stair.
Little space saved; difficult to move furniture.

Fig 5-7. Stair layouts.

Table 5-2. Riser effect on stairwell size.
8'-6" total rise, 12" floor thickness, 6'-6" minimum headroom.

No. of risers	Rise in.	Run in.	Total run	Min. floor opening
13	7⅞"	9½"	9'-6"	8'-11"
14	7¼"	10"	10'-10"	10'-4"
15	6¾"	10¾"	12'-6½"	12'-0"
16	6⅜"	11¼"	14'-¾"	13'-6"

Doors

Have doors at room corners and opening into the room, not the hall. A door that swings 90° against the wall is usually best. Have a door swing over a landing, not the descending stairs.

Pocket doors, which slide into the wall, or folding doors may fit where a conventional door cannot swing. They are useful for closets or for closing off an area for privacy or to reduce heating or cooling requirements.

Open floor plans need fewer doors. Locate remaining doors carefully for privacy and to reduce sound transmission to rooms with doors. Solid-core doors provide more privacy, useful life, and fire protection; hollow-core doors are more economical and are adequate for closets and bathrooms.

Consider the effects of exterior doors on energy efficiency. Use insulated exterior doors sealed to reduce air infiltration. Consider an airlock, Fig 5-2b. Storm doors further reduce energy flow and are recommended. Sliding glass patio door units can leak large amounts of air, so high quality is especially important. Use double pane sliding glass doors; double pane units with storm doors or the newer energy efficient glass are even better. Wood frames provide a thermal break—select steel or aluminum frames that are insulated and have a thermal break in the perimeter.

Adaptations for a Wheelchair Home

Evaluate accessibility: entrance to the home, mobility within the home, and access to the community. In general, you must be free to move about the home and reach most things needed from the wheelchair.

Provide:

• Ramps that rise no more than 1" for every 12" of run—1" in 20" is much better. Adapt slope to your abilities. Cover with a non-skid paint or surfacing material. Build landings for resting if ramp

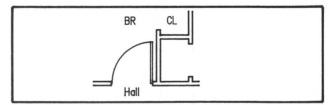

Fig 5-8. Good door location and swing.

Table 5-3. Door widths.

Door width, in.	Comments
24	Minimum for closets, half baths
30	Minimum for bedrooms, full baths
32	Recommended for all interior doors; 32" is minimum for wheelchairs
36	Recommended for exterior doors and better for wheelchairs

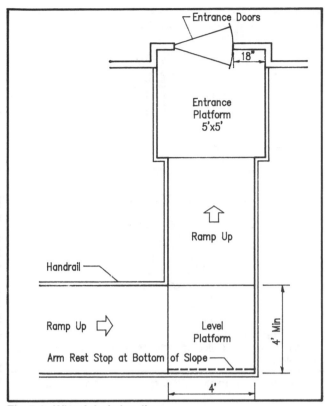

Fig 5-9. Wheelchair landing.
Provide landing for resting at a sharp change in ramp direction. Wheelchair armrest is 29″ from the ground; provide a stop to catch the chair but permit knees to pass under.

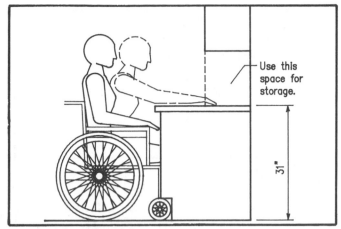

Fig 5-10. Counter and work surface height.
Consider leaving space for wheelchair to fit under sink and other critical counter areas.

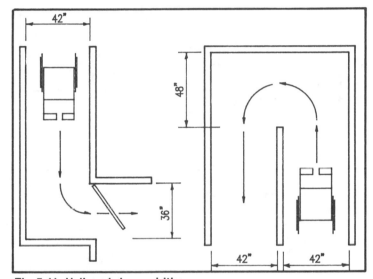

Fig 5-11. Hall and door widths.
Dimensions are minimums.

is long (every 30′, or as needed) or if the ramp changes direction. Install handrails 29″ to 32″ high. At a corner below a ramp, also install a rail to catch the chair's handrail (which is 29″ high), in case the chair rolls uncontrolled down the ramp. Use fireproof materials. See Fig 5-9.

Screening a ramp from the street provides some security. Having it visible from a window helps a person inside know if assistance is needed.

- Counters and work areas 30″ to 32″ high promote good posture and ease strain on back, shoulder and arm muscles. Fig 5-10. Consider lowering all counters if you live alone.
- Wider doors: Make entrance doors at least 36″ wide for 34″ clear opening. Make interior doors at least 32″ wide (30″ clear). See Table 5-3. Hinges are available that swing the door out of the frame and to one side to increase clear opening. Folding, swinging, cafe, and accordion doors use up some of the open space; measure before installing. Pocket doors are good, preferably without floor tracks. Remove doorsills from interior doors. Slope the edges of exterior doorsills.
- Ample floor space to maneuver. Do not let doors interfere with clear floor space. 60″x60″ is the average space suggested for a 180° or 360° turn. See Fig 5-11.
- Alcoves off the hallways are also useful, providing an area for three-point-turns where com-

plete turns are not possible. See Figs 5-12 and 5-13.

- Halls 42″ wide are minimum; 48″ is preferred.
- Hard surfaced floors: Wood or tile flooring is preferred to carpet. If carpet is used, select a low, dense pile of a durable fiber such as nylon, and install over no more than a thin pad. Test a large sample at the store. Avoid throw rugs; they are a hazard to handicapped persons on smooth-surface floors.

Pay attention to details:

- Direction doors swing.
- Door catches: easy to grasp for turning. Latches or lever-action are preferred over round knobs.
- Lights: For rooms with more than one door, provide light switches at each door. Provide lamps in every room that are low enough to permit changing bulbs from the wheelchair.

The extent of your ability and disability can be tested and measured and used when building a new home or remodeling. Rented homes often cannot be permanently altered, but some temporary modifica-

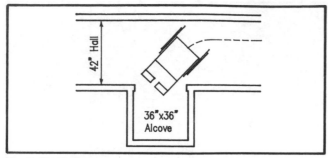

Fig 5-12. Hall alcove.
For three-point wheelchair turns.

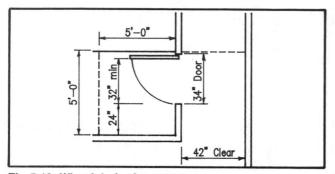

Fig 5-13. Wheelchair clearance.
To open a door, a wheelchair requires about 5′x5′ clear on the side toward which the door swings and about 42″ clear on the other side.

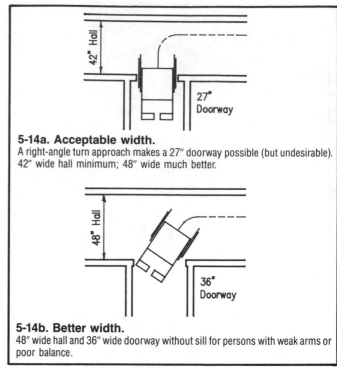

5-14a. Acceptable width.
A right-angle turn approach makes a 27″ doorway possible (but undesirable). 42″ wide hall minimum; 48″ wide much better.

5-14b. Better width.
48″ wide hall and 36″ wide doorway without sill for persons with weak arms or poor balance.

Fig 5-14. Hall and door widths for wheelchair turns.

tions of both the home and the wheelchair may be inexpensive and more functional.

Organizations and rehabilitation specialists offer information, ideas, and assistance. A few are listed below; see addresses in Chapter 20.

- Easter Seal Society—has a loan-closet program that allows individuals to borrow and experiment with various self-help items before making a purchase.
- Paralyzed Veterans of America—has published three excellent books: *Home in a Wheelchair, The Wheelchair Bathroom, The Wheelchair in the Kitchen.*
- **Accent on Living**
- Registered occupational therapists or other rehabilitation specialists. Also, engineers, architects, interior designers, or contractors experienced in barrier-free housing.

6. HOME BUSINESS CENTER

Your profession, interests, and family's life style and life cycle stage influence the type of home business center you need. This center is for home and family business: menu planning, bill paying, recordkeeping, and planning the family's social calendar. For some people it is also for family business operation, e.g. a family farm, consulting service, sewing or upholstery business, or home sales.

The activities performed define the location and relationships needed in the floor plan, the space and furnishings needed, and space arrangement. Two office/business centers are desirable for many dual career families, such as a farm operator whose spouse has a home-based business.

Location

Many home businesses need an office easily accessible to an entry; others need quiet seclusion. Some people want to be able to view their property. Natural lighting is desirable for most offices. Control glare with window treatments.

Space Requirements

Space needs depend on activities performed. A business center can be part of another room, such as living room, family room, or kitchen (along one wall and away from meal preparation). The center may be a desk with file drawer, or a separate room: 6'x6'-8" (small); 8'x10' (medium); to 10'x16' (large). See Figs 6-1 and 6-2.

To determine the required floor space, inventory your activities and equipment, as well as your file, book, and supply storage needs.

Furnishings

A calculator, computer with printer and/or typewriter, and computer-aided-design systems (CAD) require different work surfaces and heights than a writing desk. Select comfortable heights for equipment on a shelf, cabinet, table, or desk. See Fig 6-3. Select desks, counters, and tables with light to medium color work surfaces. Match storage space to need; consider height, shape, amount, and arrangement. Many desk-type units to house computer equipment and supplies (programs, etc.) are available in both wood and metal.

Seating for the work center should be adjustable to the user's size and to the opening and height of the desk. Seating for clients, workers, or family members also may be needed.

A file drawer in the desk may be adequate for filing records and resources. For separate filing systems, choose vertical or lateral file drawers. A lateral system needs only a narrow space to open, and you can choose two or more drawers high to meet your needs. See Fig 6-3a.

A two-drawer unit is about desk high. A three-drawer (counter height) unit can be a room divider. Additional drawers provide a great deal of storage or combine with other storages for a storage wall.

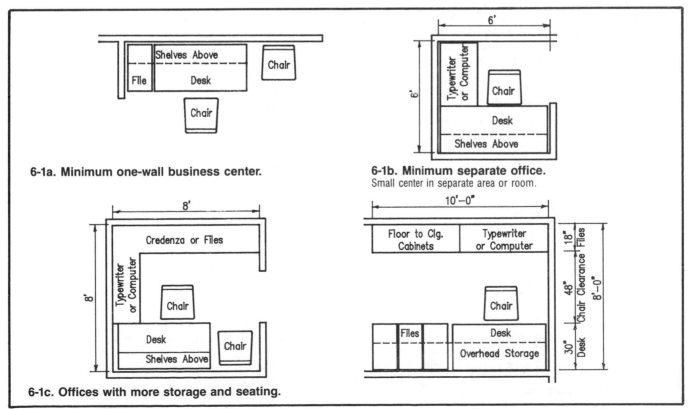

6-1a. Minimum one-wall business center.

6-1b. Minimum separate office.
Small center in separate area or room.

6-1c. Offices with more storage and seating.

Fig 6-1. Home offices.

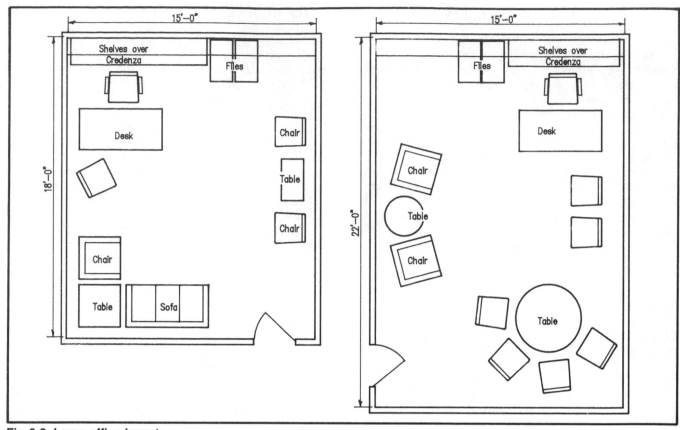

Fig 6-2. Large office layouts.
Library and business center combined. Lateral files would fit these layouts better than the more common but deeper style.

Shelves for books, etc., can be free-standing, built in, or wall hung. Shelving can be adjustable or fixed. Component storage systems are also available. Units can be mixed and matched to suit needs.

If the business center has an outdoor access or entry, provide coat storage. Consider hooks, coat/hat racks, cabinets, or a separate closet. The service entry coat closet can serve clients if the location is convenient.

Electrical Wiring and Lighting

Consider electrical needs for office equipment, lighting, and phones. Many desks and work station units conceal wiring within them. Built-ins can also conceal wiring. Concealed wiring is tidier. See Chapter 17 for information on locating electric outlets.

Consult a lighting specialist or appropriate literature for the best amount and placement of lighting. Provide for direct light on keyboard and document areas without shadows from the operator.

Arrangement

Arrange the space for convenience, which is achieved with orderly work flow. Consider all activities, items used, and communication needed to perform each activity. Identify items used most often and the most convenient place for each. Place largest items first, then smaller ones, leaving room to use each piece of equipment and to move around them.

Computer Work Stations

Provide for a flexible arrangement of keyboard, display, printer, and papers. Adjustable furniture is desirable, especially seating that adjusts for height, angle, and back support. Select glare-free general lighting; keep task or individual lighting from shining directly on the display screen.

Desirable features for comfort and convenience:
• Keyboard:
Separate from the display to allow positioning for user comfort.
Height at the middle key row: no more than 1¼″ above the desk surface.
Keyboard slope: no more than 15°.
Positioned 2″-4″ back from the front edge of the work surface.
• Display screen:
Height and angle to avoid reflections and for user comfort.
Adjustable tilt angle desirable.
Without glare or reflections.
• Document holder:
Movable, but rigid enough to write on if required.
Adjustable to an angle for comfortable posture.
Sized for the sheets to be held.
Nonreflective, to prevent glare.
• Work surface:
At least 30″ deep and 5′ wide.
Straight line, right angle, or corridor arrangements work well.
Flexible arrangement of display, keyboard, and documents is desirable.
Leg room at least 23″ wide.
Minimum height from floor: 25½″, with 27¼″ preferred.

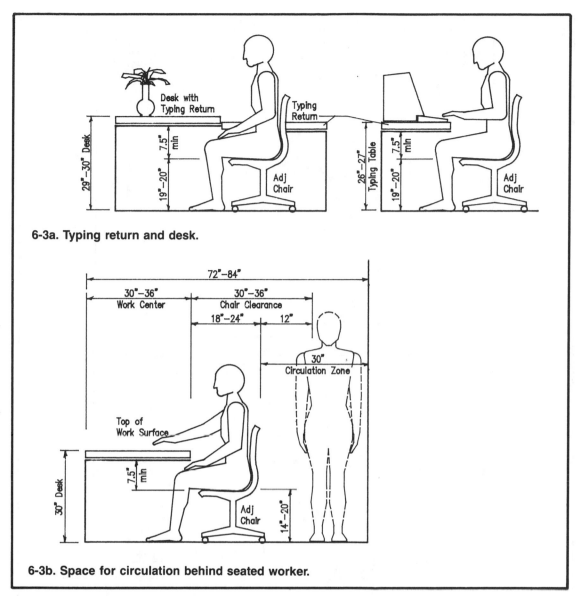

6-3a. Typing return and desk.

6-3b. Space for circulation behind seated worker.

Fig 6-3. Work center dimensions.
Desk and return should be at comfortable heights. Seating for work center adjusts to user's size.

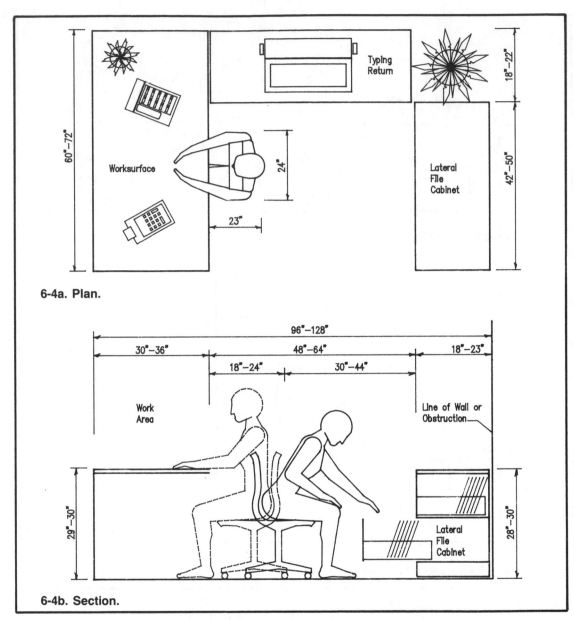

6-4a. Plan.

6-4b. Section.

Fig 6-4. U-shaped work station with back lateral file storage.

7. SOCIAL AREAS

Social areas are spaces for the family to entertain guests, relax, watch television, read, listen to music, play games, enjoy the outdoors, and eat.

Environment

A variety of activities requires a variety of rooms: family and living rooms, dining room, den, recreation room, library, music room, screened-in porch, and patio. These rooms require a large share of the space in a home. Family size, the size of groups entertained, special hobbies, and your budget determine how much space to allocate.

Good planning in single use areas such as kitchens, baths, stairs, halls, and storages leaves as much space as possible for social areas. Or, have single rooms serve more than one purpose: living-dining, living-family, kitchen-family, bath-laundry, hall-laundry, and garage-workshop. If the size and number of rooms in the social area are limited, open space or open plans can overcome feelings of confinement or smallness. Chapter 3 has more information on open plans.

Noise

Consider noise in an open plan. Isolate noisy activities from quiet ones, which may be difficult in a small house. Tight-fitting solid core doors and insulation in the walls reduce noise transmission between rooms. Avoid placing heat ducts and outlets back to back in the same wall. Carpeting, draperies, and acoustic ceiling tile help absorb sound.

Bedrooms are quiet space that can fill other needs. For example, bedrooms can be for television viewing or a spot to study and practice musical instruments, while a party is in the dining-living-family area.

Dust and Odors

Manage kitchen and bath odors and moisture with good exhaust fans. Control dust from hobbies such as woodworking with isolation. Chapter 2 discusses outdoor noise and odors.

Location

The social area is the core of the house. A central location lets traffic "fan out" to other areas. Provide a separate entry in the social area connecting inside and outside living areas. If you entertain with outdoor cooking, have the kitchen near the patio door, screened-in porch, or backyard.

Arrangement

Avoid cross traffic through the center of social areas. Notice in Fig 7-1 the good and poor entrance locations in a living room. In the poor plan, people walking through interfere with conversation or television viewing. It is better to group the doorways at a corner or have the traffic lane across one end of the room. Avoid through traffic in smaller living rooms.

Size

The ideal conversation circle for seated people is about 10' in diameter. In Fig 7-2a., the people on the couch and those on the chairs tend to make two small groups, rather than one large one. For standing people, such as at parties, the natural conversation circle is about 6'. With a room 12'-14' wide, furniture along each side of the room is the proper distance apart. Avoid living area widths greater than 14' unless there is a traffic lane along one side, or unless the extra width has furniture that is not part of the conversation circle.

It is easier to arrange furniture in rectangular rooms than square ones. One conversation circle with extra space for circulation requires a room 16'-18' long. A 22' long room holds two conversation circles.

Alter the suggested sizes to match each family's individual activities. A versatile living room can be multi-purpose.

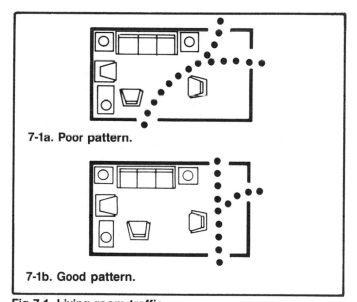

7-1a. Poor pattern.

7-1b. Good pattern.

Fig 7-1. Living room traffic.
Poor doorway location creates traffic lanes through the conversation area.

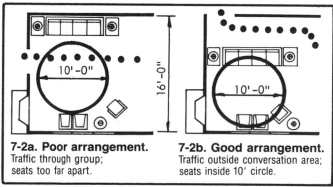

7-2a. Poor arrangement.
Traffic through group; seats too far apart.

7-2b. Good arrangement.
Traffic outside conversation area; seats inside 10' circle.

Fig 7-2. Conversation circle.

Table 7-1. Living room furniture areas.
Allow 18"-24" between a sofa or chair and a coffee table. Clearance needed at a rocker or recliner varies.

Furniture	Dimensions
2-person sofa	32" or 34" deep
	50", 55", 60" long
3-person sofa	32" or 34" deep
	72" to 102" long
Straight back armchair	27" or 29" deep
	27" long
Rocking chair	22"x24"
Recliner/rocker	30"x29" (66"-75" open)

Storage

Effective storage makes a multipurpose room more usable. List all the room's uses and plan storage for all items needed. Hidden storage can be especially useful. Built-in storage is always ready for use and can be easily concealed by folding doors or shutters. See the storage chapter for more ideas.

Family Room

Many houses have a family room. It permits separating active (informal) and passive (formal) activities. Consider the living room for conversation, reading, music, and studying and the family room for games, dancing, hobbies, and active play. The stereo might be in the living room and television in the family room.

Family rooms vary so much with individuals that guidelines are not well established. A space smaller than 12'x16' is not recommended, but family rooms can be much larger (14'x18' for pool table). Decide what your family wants to do there and refer to other chapters of this handbook for space requirements.

Great Room

The term **great room** sometimes means living room, but more often it means a large dining-living-family-kitchen multipurpose area. Great rooms seem well suited for smaller families who entertain large groups in a smaller house. Some people like to keep contact with the family while on "kitchen duty". Large families may find a great room noisy for day-to-day living and too public for individual activities. Fireplaces and dividers can break the room into smaller areas.

Special Activity Spaces

Some rooms serve particular hobbies or interests, and are part of the social area. Special interests vary, so plan size and shape for your needs. As you plan your "special room":
- Avoid a traffic lane through the room.
- Avoid a line-of-sight view from the guest entry or living room if this room may appear cluttered.
- Isolate the room by construction or distance if noise or odors from your activities may be objectionable to the rest of the house or vice versa.
- Plan for needed storage.
- Consider special floor coverings, an exhaust fan, separate temperature control, and other space and facility features to support the activities.

8. DINING AREAS

Plan eating space according to family needs and preferences. Provide adequate dining space for the number of people you wish to serve at one time. Allow space for the table, other furniture, and for moving around the room while people are seated.

Space from table to wall or other furniture:
- 32″ to push chair back and rise.
- 36″ to edge past seated person.
- 44″ to walk past seated person.

For eating family meals in the kitchen, locate space outside, but convenient to, the food preparation area.

A snack bar or eating counter may be convenient if there is enough room for both the counter and the chairs, Fig 8-1. A counter is not as flexible as a table but may take less floor space.

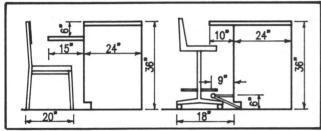

Fig 8-1. Eating counters.
Use chairs with counter at table height on a base cabinet.
Use stools or taller chairs with counters that are more than 30″ high. Stools are less safe and convenient for children and older people.

Many families want a separate dining room. If space is limited, a dining-living area allows expansion of the table yet reduces the space set aside for dining, Fig 8-2.

Provide adequate room length and width, Fig 8-3 to 8-6. Areas are given in the captions for comparison.

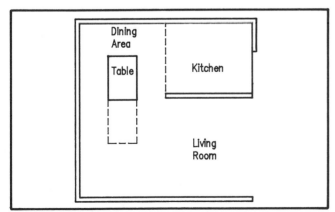

Fig 8-2. Dining space expanding into living room.

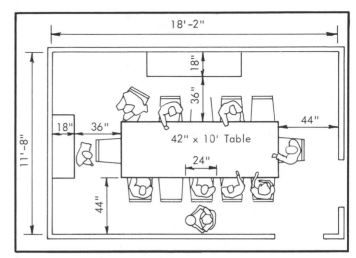

Fig 8-3. A dining room for 12.
A hutch or buffet is typically about 18″ deep. A 42″ wide table is common. There is space behind the chairs to edge past one side and one end, and to walk past on the other side and end. Table space is 24″ per person, the minimum place setting zone. With arm chairs at the ends, allow an extra 2″ for each; add 4″ to the room length.

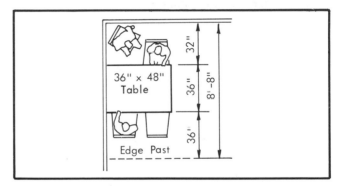

Fig 8-4. Minimum width for table and chairs.
8′-8″ for 36″ wide table, 32″ on one side to rise from the table and 36″ on the other side to edge past. A 48″ long table seats 4 and requires 34.6 ft².

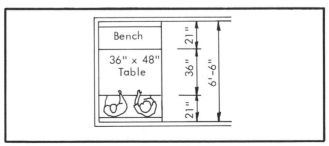

Fig 8-5. Dining space with benches.
6′-6″ for benches on both sides of a 36″ table. A 48″ long table seats 4 and requires 26 ft².

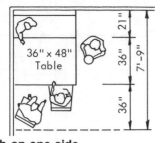

8-6a. Bench on one side.
7'-9" for a bench on one side and chairs on the other. Seating for four requires 31 ft².

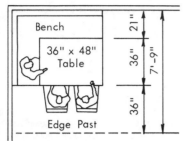

8-6b. Corner bench.
Benches on one side and one end, and two chairs on the other side, seat five at a 3'x4' table in 44.5 ft².

Fig 8-6. Bench and chair dining.

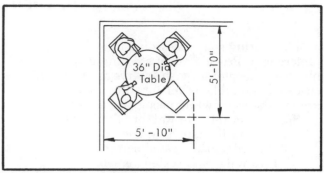

Fig 8-7. Round tables.
A 36" round table with four swivel chairs fit in a 5'-10"x5'-10" or 34 ft² corner space.

A round table usually does not save space, but it may fit a small space better than a rectangular table. See Table 8-1.

Table 8-1. Round table seating.

Diameter of round table	No. of seats
36"	4
42"	5
48"	6

9. KITCHENS

Whether you are planning a new kitchen or evaluating an existing kitchen, consider the principles presented in this chapter.

Location

The kitchen is often the center of daily operations. From it, many trips are made to other parts of the house and to outside areas. Keep inside traffic routes reasonably short. When locating the kitchen, see Fig 9-1 and consider the following routes and suggestions:

- To the guest entry: direct and not through the living room conversation area.
- To the service entry: direct, but avoid the meal preparation area.
- To bedrooms, bath, and laundry: when dovetailing kitchen work with other homemaking activities, avoid traffic through the living and family rooms.
- To serve food outdoors: avoid the garage and laundry room.
- To serve food in a separate dining room: direct path from the kitchen.

Consider the kitchen relative to:

- External light. East windows help make a kitchen bright in the morning. North windows usually eliminate glare, but limit size to reduce heat loss.
- Solar heating. Because the kitchen has heat generating appliances, late afternoon direct solar gain through west windows is undesirable year round. Avoid west windows in the kitchen.
- View. Important views may be scenery, the children's play area, the driveway to see who is approaching, and on the farm, a view of the farm court and buildings.
- Life style. Kitchen location and size are affected by how you use the kitchen area.

Planning

Good kitchen planning is based on "centers", which are combined for logical flow of activities performed in the kitchen. The usual centers are refrigeration, mixing, sink, cooking/baking, microwave oven, and planning. Some references include a serving center, but it is usually the counter space in the cooking/baking area.

When combining centers into complete kitchen plans, keep in mind the logical work progression during meal preparation, Fig 9-2.

Fig 9-3 shows a good arrangement of the centers and how they may overlap. Right handed persons work most efficiently from right to left with the refrigerator at the right end and the sink at the left end of the mixing center. Left-handed persons typically prefer the reverse. Most people, however, adapt readily to either progression if the centers relate correctly with each other.

Figs 9-5 through 9-9 show recommended dimensions for the various centers.

Refrigerator Center

Meal preparation frequently begins at the refrigerator-freezer, where perishables needed at the mixing center are stored. Many items also go directly from the refrigerator to the table.

- Allow a 36″ wide space for the refrigerator regardless of size of your present unit. See Fig 9-6.
- Provide at least 15″ of counter next to the latch side of the refrigerator door.
- If a refrigerator-freezer is near a corner, Fig 9-5a, install the appliance with at least one foot of counter before the corner, to avoid stepping back from the door. Have the door swing away from work spaces.

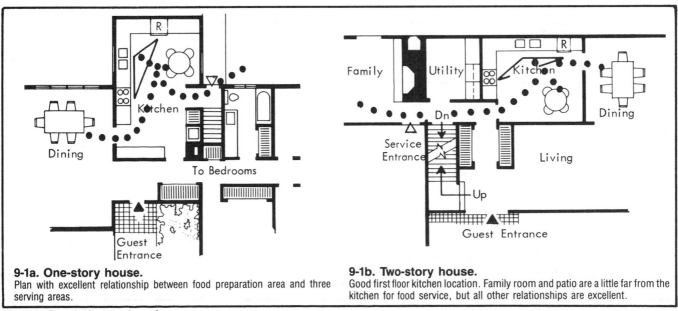

9-1a. One-story house.
Plan with excellent relationship between food preparation area and three serving areas.

9-1b. Two-story house.
Good first floor kitchen location. Family room and patio are a little far from the kitchen for food service, but all other relationships are excellent.

Fig 9-1. Good kitchen locations.

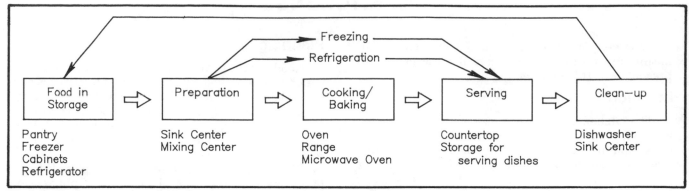

Fig 9-2. Meal preparation work flow.

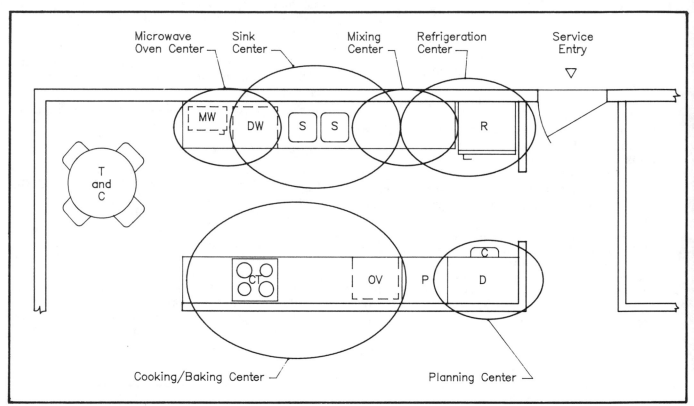

Fig 9-3. Kitchen centers.
Centers may overlap and share counter space.

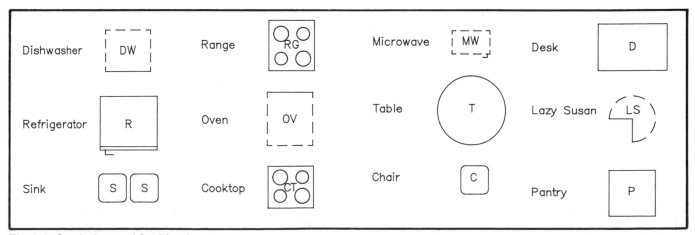

Fig 9-4. Symbols used in this chapter.

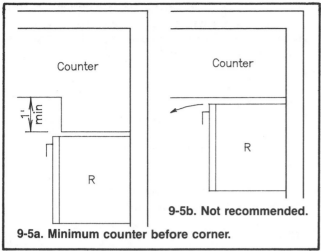

9-5b. Not recommended.

9-5a. Minimum counter before corner.

Fig 9-5. Refrigerator location.

Mixing Center

On this section of counter, ingredients are brought together for preparation before going to the range, oven, microwave oven, or table.

• Provide 48″ to 54″ of counter space, preferably between refrigerator and sink. See Fig 9-6 and recommendations for refrigeration and sink centers.

• Provide at least 36″ of counter space if mixing center must be elsewhere in the kitchen.

• Provide storage above and below the mixing counter for staple supplies, spices, mixing bowls, portable appliances, etc.

Sink Center

Water is used for both food preparation, such as washing fresh vegetables, and for cooking on the range or in the microwave oven. A central location is important. See Figs 9-3 and 9-6.

• Preferably between refrigerator and range.

• Provide about 36″ of counter space on one side for stacking dirty dishes and 24″-30″ on the other side for clean dishes.

• Most people prefer double-bowl sinks, even with a dishwasher.

• A 32″ double-bowl sink fits a 36″ sink base cabinet.

• A single-bowl sink fits a 30″ sink base cabinet.

• Standard dishwashers are 24″ wide, 24″ deep, and 34½″ high. In Fig 9-6, a built-in dishwasher would be to the left of the sink.

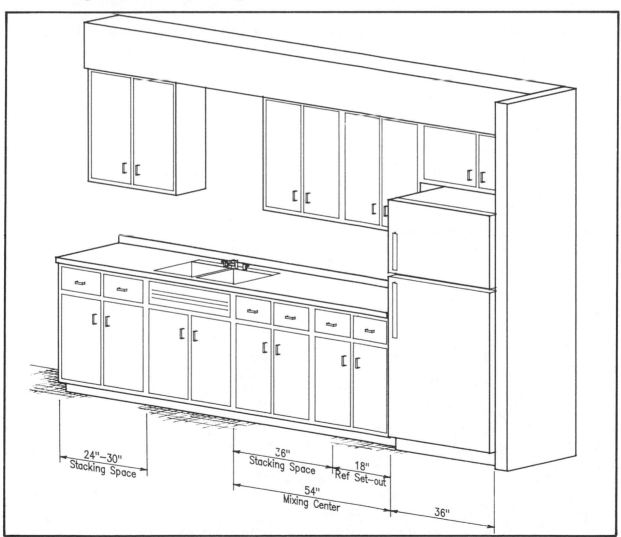

Fig 9-6. Combined space for sink, mixing center, and refrigerator set-out.

- Preferably put the dishwasher next to the sink. Or, put it just around the corner from the sink, allowing enough space so the open dishwasher door does not interfere with sink access. Put the dishwasher left of the sink for right-handed workers and right of the sink for left-handed workers.
- If the dishwasher is near a corner, be sure the handle clears adjacent cabinet handles. Beware of leaving a corner cabinet that you cannot access for storage.

Cooking/Baking Center

Food ready for cooking or baking usually goes to a range, oven, or microwave oven. See Fig 9-7. See also, Microwave Cooking Center.

- Locate center near daily eating area for convenient serving.
- Provide 18″-24″ counter space on both sides of cooking surface. This counter is sometimes called the serving center. Store serving bowls and platters above or below the counter.
- Next to a wall oven, provide 18″-24″ counter space, which may be the same space provided next to the cooktop, as in Fig 9-7.

Ranges

- A range requires less kitchen wall space than a cooktop and separate oven.

- If counter space is limited, a 30″ range is a better choice than a wider one or separate units.
- Do not install a range or cooktop below a window or with a side against a wall.

Ovens

- Oven cabinets come 24″, 27″, 30″, and 33″ wide.
- Select ovens (conventional and microwave) before planning the kitchen so the correct width cabinet can be installed.
- For safety, put the bottom of the oven no higher than 36″.
- When oven and microwave oven are one above the other, put the microwave 42″ to 50″ above the floor with the conventional oven below it.

Microwave Cooking Center

Consider the following when locating a microwave oven:

- Leave space around the microwave for cooling and venting.
- Preferred location is near the mix and refrigerator centers. With a door hinged on the left, it may be left of a counter section. See Fig 9-8.
- A satisfactory location is above a wall oven if height is controlled. It may be a little far from the mix center depending on kitchen arrangement. See Fig 9-7.

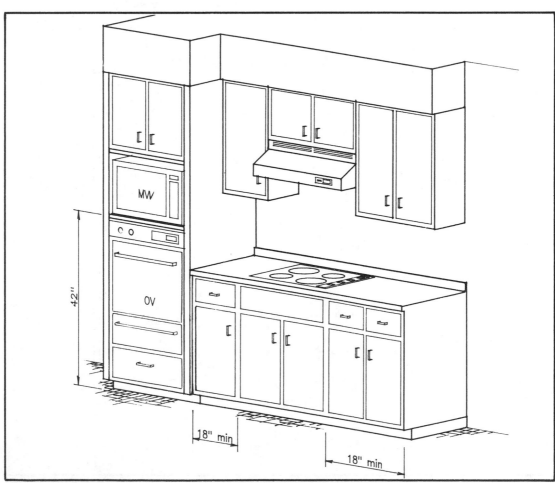

Fig 9-7. Cooking/baking center with microwave oven.

- A location above the range is inconvenient when two persons work in the kitchen; is too high for most people to remove hot foods safely; is a hazard when reaching across steaming cooking utensils on the surface below; and restricts vertical space for large pots on cooktops.
- Another option is to put the microwave oven on a cart.

The best surface height on which to set a microwave oven is:

- For convenience: elbow height plus or minus 6″. The standard 42″ surface height is recommended because it accommodates elbow heights from 36″-48″, which includes most people from 5′-0″ to 6′-2″ tall.
- For safety: 3″ below shoulder height. A 50″ maximum is suggested, because a house may be occupied by a series of people of varying heights. For adults 5′-0″ to 6′-2″ tall, shoulder height is typically 49″-61″.

Planning Center

Provide space in the kitchen to plan meals, use the telephone, and perhaps keep family financial records.

- See desk and chair locations in Fig 9-10.
- It can be a built-in or movable desk about 36″ wide and 18″-24″ deep.
- Writing surface may be 29″ high with a chair or 36″ high with a bar stool or tall chair.
- Consider space for a microcomputer.

- Provide storage for cook books, writing supplies, telephone books, etc.

Combining Centers into Complete Kitchens

The counter spaces with each center serve more than one function when centers are combined, as shown in Fig 9-3. Fig 9-9 shows dimensions of overlapping centers. When a kitchen arrangement turns a corner, the 2′x2′ square of counter in the corner is not "frontage"; even though it is available for storage, it is less convenient for working.

One measure of kitchen efficiency is the work triangle. The perimeter of the work triangle measured between center fronts of the refrigerator, sink, and range should not be less than 15′ or greater than 23′. The work triangle does not allow for steps to reach a microwave or conventional wall oven, or a pantry storage. Consider your food preparation preferences and make access to these items as convenient as possible.

Each of the four kitchens shown in Fig 9-10 has the following features:

- A work triangle perimeter within 15′-23′ for efficiency.
- Work centers with at least minimum counter space.
- Recommended work center locations for good work flow, Fig 9-2: refrigerator to mixing to sink to cooking/baking.

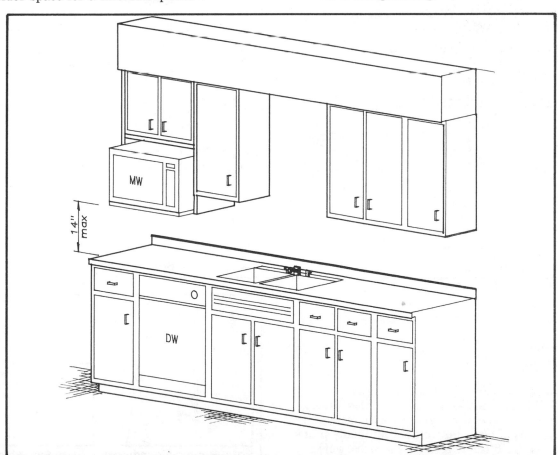

Fig 9-8. Microwave oven center.
Microwave oven may set on a 36″ high counter or on a shelf no more than 50″ high. Small microwaves may be mounted under a wall cabinet.

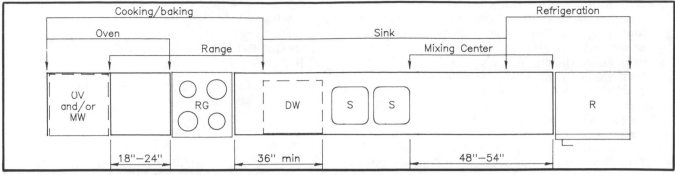

Fig 9-9. Minimum counter frontage.
For combined work centers.

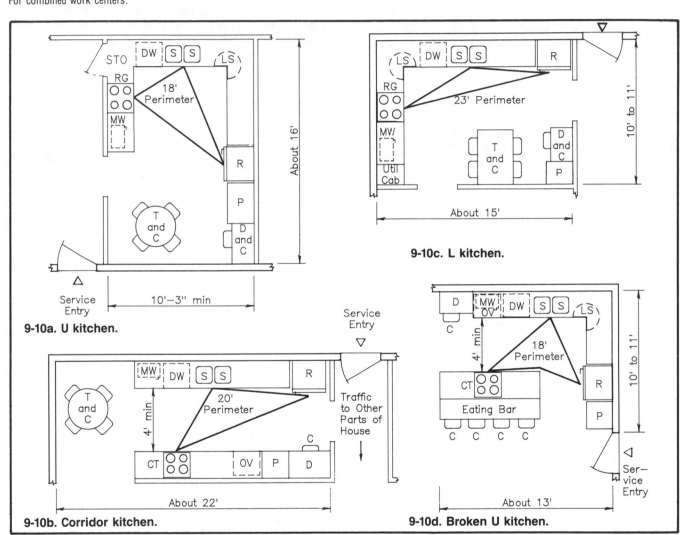

9-10a. U kitchen.

9-10b. Corridor kitchen.

9-10c. L kitchen.

9-10d. Broken U kitchen.

Fig 9-10. Four basic kitchens.

- Microwave cooking center in convenient location.
- Planning center.
- Dining space.
- Pantry cabinet.
- No traffic through the work triangle.

These kitchens represent a variety of layouts. Reverse each plan for left-to-right work sequence. By moving features of one plan to another, many plans can be created with the desired appliances, working surfaces, and storage space to make meal preparation and serving efficient.

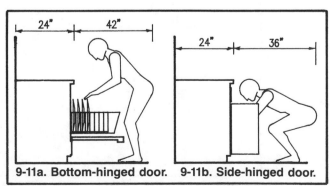

9-11a. Bottom-hinged door. 9-11b. Side-hinged door.

Fig 9-11. Free space needed to use appliances.

Fig 9-11 shows free floor space needed to use kitchen appliances comfortably. This space is automatically provided if minimum dimensions in Fig 9-10 can be met.

Cabinets

Kitchen cabinets are readily available in widths that vary by 3″ and 6″ increments. Pre-finished filler strips or adjustable blind corner cabinets are available to fill uneven wall space dimensions.

Base cabinets
• The standard height is 36″ with the counter top. Customize for a lower or higher work surface only if you expect to use the kitchen for many years. The next user may not be the same height.
• Standard cabinet depth is 24″.
• Pull-out trays make things more accessible than fixed shelves.
• Fit at least one base cabinet with drawers of various depths.
• A lap board 27″ above the floor is nice for sit-down work.
• Pull-out chopping and pastry boards are handy.
• A lazy Susan makes corner space more usable.

Wall cabinets
• Wall cabinets are 12″-42″ high and 12″ deep.
• 30″ high cabinets are usually 18″ above the counter, so from floor to soffit is 7′. Cabinets, rather than a soffit, provide storage for seldom-used items.
• 33″ high cabinets mounted 15″ above the counter give the same overall height but lower the shelf heights for easier access.
• Adjustable shelves are useful.
• To reduce injuries on open doors, avoid cabinet doors wider than 16″. Double doors on 36″ wide cabinets are about 16″ wide. Infrequently used cabinets could have wider doors.

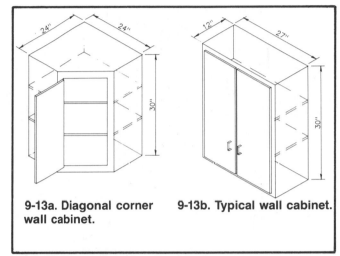

9-13a. Diagonal corner wall cabinet.   **9-13b. Typical wall cabinet.**

Fig 9-13. Examples of wall cabinets.

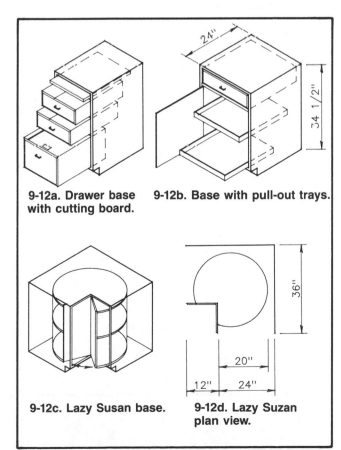

9-12a. Drawer base with cutting board.   **9-12b. Base with pull-out trays.**

9-12c. Lazy Susan base.   **9-12d. Lazy Suzan plan view.**

Fig 9-12. Base cabinets with convenience features.

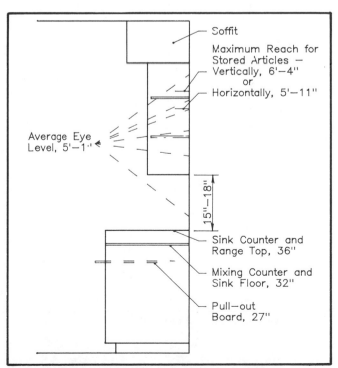

Soffit

Maximum Reach for Stored Articles — Vertically, 6'-4" or Horizontally, 5'-11"

Average Eye Level, 5'-1"

Sink Counter and Range Top, 36"

Mixing Counter and Sink Floor, 32"

Pull-out Board, 27"

Fig 9-14. Suggested kitchen surface heights.

9.8

Tall cabinets
- Oven, pantry, and utility cabinets are 84″ high and 12″-24″ deep, Fig 9-15.
- Choose oven cabinets with openings no more than 50″ high for a microwave oven.

- Mount conventional ovens lower than microwave ovens for easier handling of heavier items, such as a turkey.
- For easy visibility, consider 12″ rather than 24″ deep utility cabinets for storage.

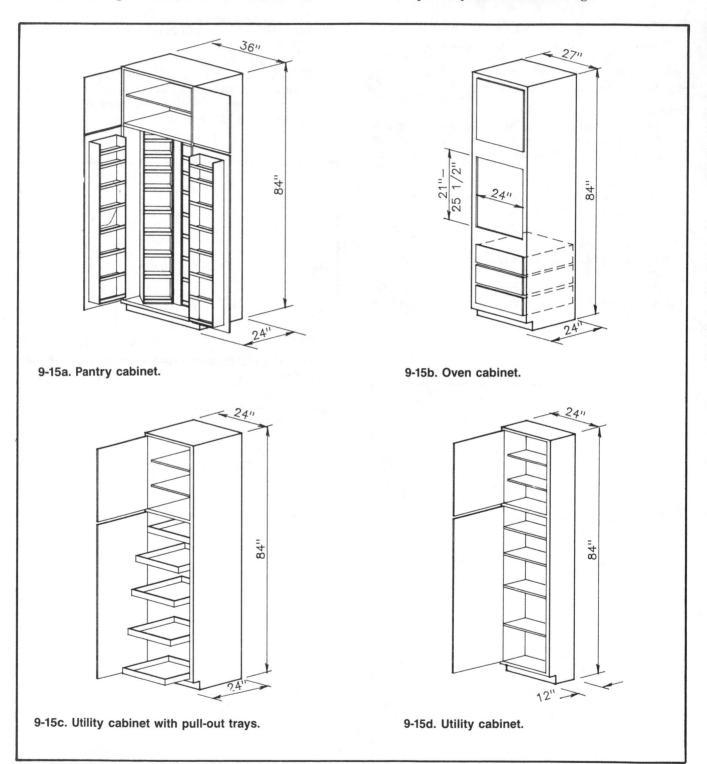

9-15a. Pantry cabinet.

9-15b. Oven cabinet.

9-15c. Utility cabinet with pull-out trays.

9-15d. Utility cabinet.

Fig 9-15. Examples of tall cabinets.

10. CLOTHES CARE

Planning for clothes care—laundry, mending, etc.—makes the work easier and more efficient. First list all of your activities, the equipment needed, and the amount of space required. The list will help you plan space in your home to best satisfy your needs, Table 10-1.

Most of the activities in Table 10-1 could be accommodated in a room about 8' × 15' as shown in Fig 10-1. The equipment, work surfaces, and storage are arranged so work progresses in a logical sequence to reduce the time and energy needed.

This complete clothes care center combines the sewing and laundry centers. It encourages combining mending, pressing, and laundering. The laundry

sorting and folding table doubles for cutting fabrics for sewing. If necessary or desirable to separate laundry and sewing centers, study the sections that follow.

Laundry Center

Location

Choose the best location and layout that fits your activities, living pattern, budget, and available finances. For drying laundry outside, convenient outdoor access is important. Provide floor drain if possible. See Fig 10-2.

Sleeping area. Most soiled linens and clothing collect here, and most clean clothing and linens are stored here, so consider this location. Laundry equipment is not silent, so you may not want it running next to your bedroom. A separate room is highly desirable, especially for a complete clothes care center.

First floor utility and/or mudroom. This area eliminates stair climbing, allows for messiness, and if near the kitchen, permits supervising activities in both areas at the same time. Provide direct outside access for mudroom, cleanup, or gardening functions.

Kitchen. Consider laundering here for ease of doing several tasks at once. For sanitation, separate food preparation space from laundry work space and storage.

Basement. The laundry center is often in the basement because of less demand on space. Leaks or overflows are less apt to damage floor coverings. Other advantages are less noise in the rest of the

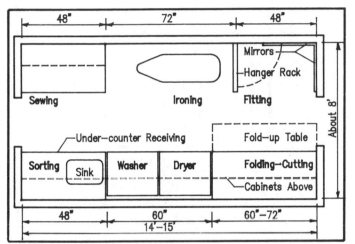

Fig 10-1. Work flow in a complete clothes care center.

Table 10-1. Clothes care activities list.

Activities performed	Equipment needed	Space
Store soiled clothing	Hamper(s)	Under counter
Sort soiled clothing	Table/shelf	Counter and sink, 24"x48", 32" high
Pretreat soiled clothing	Sink	
Machine wash and dry	Washer and dryer	Minimum 5'-0" with 3' in front for washer/dryer
Hand wash	Sink	Same as pretreat sink
Drip dry	Hanging rack	May be over bathtub to collect drip
	Clothes lines	If hanging load of clothes outdoors, 40'-50' of line with 2' between lines for passage
Fold and hang clean, dry clothes	Table/shelf	24"x72" is desirable. Can be same area as sorting counter plus top of washer/dryer and hooks for clothes on hangers
Iron	Iron and ironing boards, hampers, and other equipment	About 4'x6' floor space. Place to hang board
Prepare fabrics for sewing	Table/counter/shelf	36"x60"-72" table or 24"x60" with drop leaf desirable
Design/layout/cut		Counter
Construct/sew	Sewing machine and other equipment	4' counter for sewing
Fit	Full length mirror	
Press	Iron/ironing board	

house and access to hot water and other plumbing lines. There are two disadvantages: It is difficult to combine laundering with other activities, and many trips up and down the stairs become part of laundering. A 16"x16" laundry chute from the upper floors saves trips.

Others. Hall, closet, or pantry locations are possible, but space is usually inadequate for sorting and folding.

Space Requirements

An efficient laundry area accommodates the activities related to clothing and soiled linens shown in

Fig 10-3. The sequence of tasks is as important for laundry as for meal preparation. Fig 10-3 shows the natural work flow for laundry processes. Fig 10-4 is a good layout.

Laundry preparation requires sink access, sorting space, containers for dirty clothes, and storage for pretreatment supplies and equipment. Sorting a 32-lb wash can be on a 6' long table at a comfortable height. Or, sort into three to six bins or baskets as clothes accumulate.

Store detergents, water conditioners, fabric softeners, bleaches, measures, and stain removers near

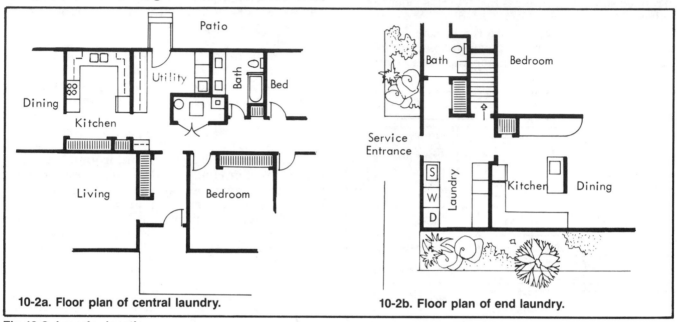

10-2a. Floor plan of central laundry.

10-2b. Floor plan of end laundry.

Fig 10-2. Laundry location.

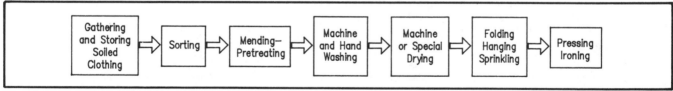

Fig 10-3. Work flow in laundry.

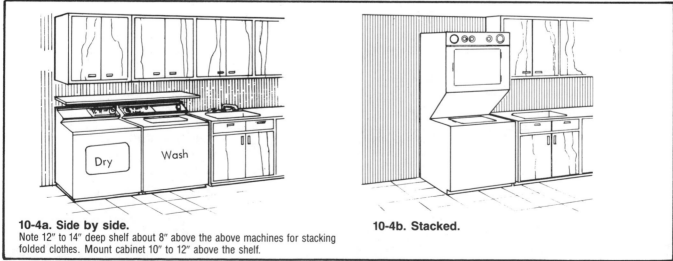

10-4a. Side by side.
Note 12" to 14" deep shelf about 8" above the above machines for stacking folded clothes. Mount cabinet 10" to 12" above the shelf.

10-4b. Stacked.

Fig 10-4. Washer and dryer.

the washing machine, but out of the reach of children. See the storage chapter for storage depths required.

A non-automatic washer, rinse tubs, and work space require about 8'x8'. The locations of drains and agitator controls influence the best arrangement.

Automatic washers are 24″-30″ wide. Leave room above a top opening washer for opening the lid and loading clothes. Front opening washers require space for the door to open and for the worker to bend.

Put the dryer near the washer and where it can be vented to the outdoors. For handicapped access, leave space between the appliances for easier loading, unloading, and reaching controls. Dryers are 24″-30″ wide. If space is limited, stack models and combination washer-dryers are available. Provide at least 36″ in front of the dryer. Provide a folding table and clothes rods near the dryer. A laundry cart and clothes pins are useful for line drying.

Hang no-iron garments as they come from the dryer. Fold on a 24″x60″ table or on the tops of the machines, and stack folded items on a shelf above the folding space, Fig 10-4.

Provide about 4'-3″x6' of floor space for using an ironing board—30″ on the working side, 6″ on the

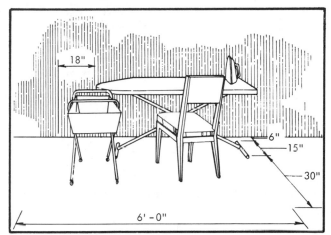

Fig 10-5. Ironing space requirements.

back, and 18″ at the point of the board, Fig 10-5. A built-in or commercial board that folds against the wall saves space. Allow space for dampening and for stacking and hanging unpressed and pressed clothes within easy reach. Store spray starch etc., nearby.

The sinks, counter, and storage space may also make the clothes care area convenient for activities such as photography and house plant care.

Sewing Centers

An efficient sewing center accommodates the activities in Fig 10-6 and space for mending, storing supplies, and stacking and hanging garments.

Location

Consider how much and when the sewing is done, and the space available for the sewing center.

If much of the family's clothing and textile furnishings are made at home, develop a well organized sewing center. If sewing dovetails with meal preparation or supervising children, put sewing near the kitchen; for evening sewing, in or near the family room may be your choice. Other locations for the sewing center are a bedroom (preferably a spare one), the basement, the second floor or as part of a complete clothes-care center.

Space Requirements

Pattern alteration and cutting. A surface 3' or more wide, 6' long, and 35″-38″ high is desirable. Provide work space on at least two sides, Fig 10-7. Options include:
- A drop-leaf table.
- A 2' wide cabinet with fold-up top.
- A drop-down or lift-up wall unit.
- A large table.

Machine sewing. Allow 2'x5' for a cabinet sewing machine plus space to sit, Fig 10-8. A portable machine on a table or counter may need more or less space. Also allow space for pressing.

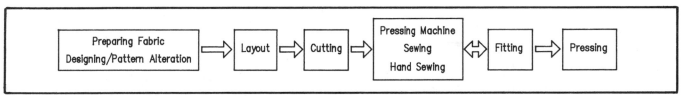

Fig 10-6. Work flow in clothing construction.

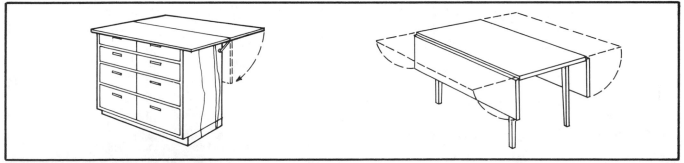

Fig 10-7. Sewing center cutting tables.
Also, folding area for clean clothing.

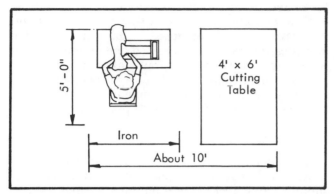

Fig 10-8. Sewing space requirements.

Hand sewing. Hand sewing at the sewing machine or ironing board needs no additional space. For hand sewing in a more comfortable chair or at a table, plan additional space.

Storage

Store tools and supplies in drawers or on shelves near the sewing machine or in separate storage for a portable machine. Provide hanging space for garments being made or needing mending. Fig 10-9 shows storage closets for sewing supplies.

Many sewing processes can be done while seated. Arrange supplies and equipment within reach of the chair. A swivel (stenographer's) chair is convenient.

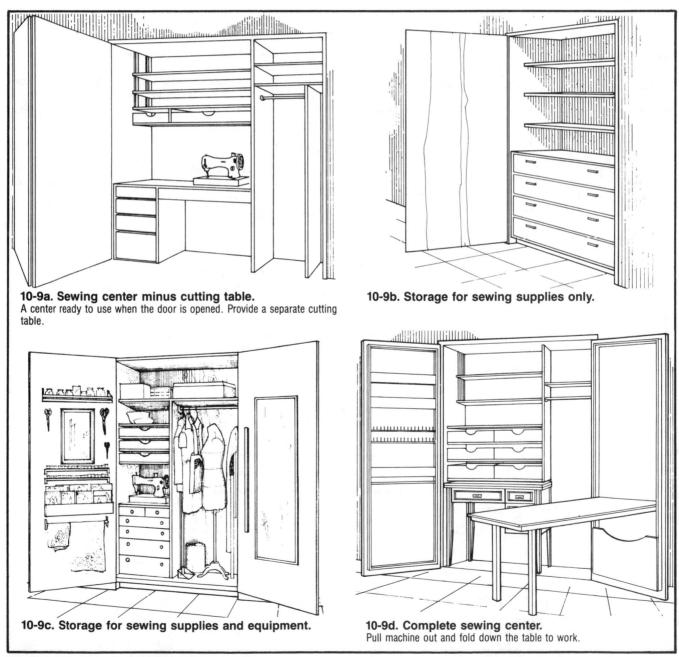

10-9a. Sewing center minus cutting table.
A center ready to use when the door is opened. Provide a separate cutting table.

10-9b. Storage for sewing supplies only.

10-9c. Storage for sewing supplies and equipment.

10-9d. Complete sewing center.
Pull machine out and fold down the table to work.

Fig 10-9. Storage closets for sewing supplies.

11. BATHROOMS

Bathrooms provide space and facilities for grooming and health care. Careful planning, good workmanship, and quality materials and fixtures provide the most convenience, satisfaction, safety, and freedom from maintenance.

Location

Generally, follow these guidelines:
- Avoid bathrooms visible from guest entry or living area.
- Avoid bathrooms opening off the kitchen or dining room, where food is prepared and eaten.
- Minimize sound transmission.
- In multistory houses, one bathroom above another minimizes plumbing requirements. Allow for water and waste lines between upstairs and basement.

In a one-bathroom house:
- Locate bathroom centrally to serve all bedrooms, Fig 10-2a.
- Locate bathroom for easy access from service entry without interfering with living area.

In multiple bathroom houses:
- Locate one bathroom centrally, as in one-bathroom houses.
- Locate others for: privacy for master bedroom; dual purposes, such as master bedroom and service entry, Fig 11-1; and other floors in a multistory house.

Bathroom Planning

Base your bathroom planning decisions on:
- Family size.
- Ages and sex of children.
- Family activities such as swimming and sunbathing.
- Budget.

Fig 11-2 shows adequate space for all fixtures, although some spaces shown are minimum. None of the examples allows generous space. If you can afford and want extra space, expand the size.

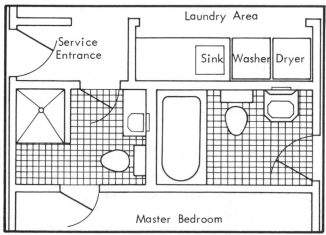

Fig 11-1. Master bedroom bath arrangement.

Each full and compartmented bathroom has a 32" wide door, which is minimum for a wheelchair (34" door is better), which is recommended for at least one

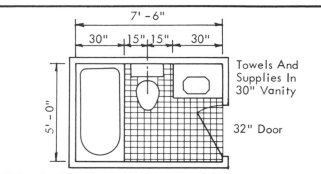

11-2a. Small, 3-fixture bathroom.
A small 3-fixture bathroom with limited storage in a built-in vanity meets basic bathroom requirements in a space 37.5 ft². The door is 32" wide for a person with a cane or crutches. This bathroom is too small for a wheelchair.

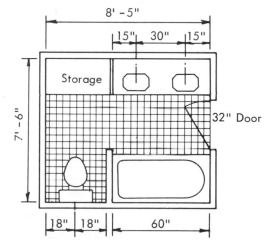

11-2b. Two-lavatory bathroom.
A 2-lavatory bathroom with adequate room at the toilet and each lavatory. Note storage space under the lavatories and in a floor-to-ceiling unit. Area: 63 ft².

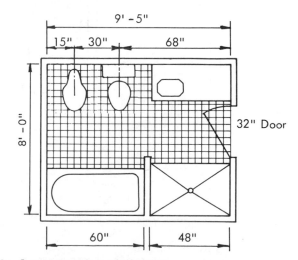

11-2c. Separate tub and shower.
This plan also includes a bidet. Storage is in the 48" long vanity. Area: 75.3 ft².

Fig 11-2. Twelve bathroom arrangements.

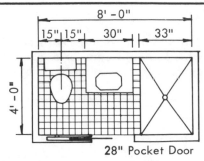

28" Pocket Door

11-2d. Large shower.
A generous 33"x48" shower is featured in this 32 ft² bathroom. Storage is under the 30" vanity and on shelves over the toilet.

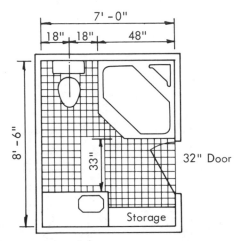

32" Door

Storage

11-2e. Corner square tub.
Although not usually a space saver, a square tub fits some situations better than a rectangular one. This 3-fixture bathroom has excellent storage but is only 59.5 ft².

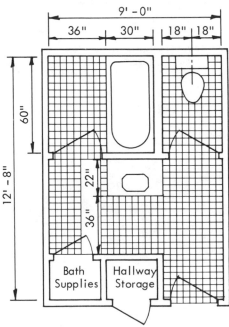

Bath Supplies   **Hallway Storage**

11-2f. Large 3-fixture bathroom.
With fixtures in separate compartments, this layout can replace a second bath by accommodating more than one person at a time. It is as large as two bathrooms but costs less because of fewer fixtures and less plumbing. Area: 106 ft² plus hallway storage.

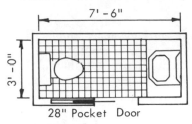

28" Pocket Door

11-2g. Generous half-bath.
22.5 ft² is a generous half-bath. A wall-hung lavatory instead of a vanity squeezes into 2'-6" width and 16.3 ft².

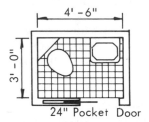

24" Pocket Door

11-2h. Corner toilet in a half-bath.
A corner toilet and a small lavatory fit 13.5 ft². Consider this idea for installing a half-bath in a closet or under a stairway.

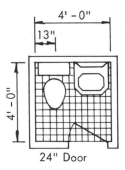

24" Door

11-2i. Minimum half-bath.
16 ft² is about minimum for standard fixtures; 4'-6"x4'-6" gives a more spacious feeling.

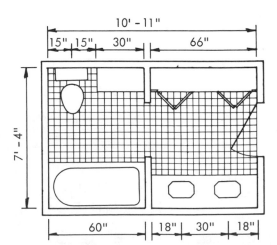

11-2j. Four-fixtures, two compartments.
Three people can use this bathroom at the same time. Consider a pocket door between the compartments. Even with generous storage space it takes only the same space as many non-compartmented bathrooms, about 80.5 ft².

Fig 11-2. Twelve bathroom arrangements continued.

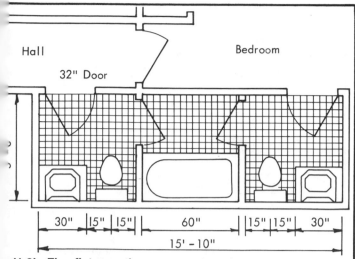

11-2k. Five fixtures, three compartments.
This bathroom serves as two full bathrooms in 87 ft². Two doors to each compartment are undesirable. Limited storage space available.

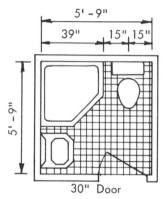

11-2l. Corner shower.
A corner shower, toilet, and lavatory fit in 33 ft². Very little storage space available.

Fig 11-2. Twelve bathroom arrangements continued.

Fig 11-3. Lavatory in closet.

bathroom on the main floor in every house. Narrower doors are acceptable for second and third bathrooms. Consider doors that swing out from a bath, which is being recommended by some codes to permit easier rescue of someone fallen against the door. Also consider a pocket door.

Planning Considerations Other Than Space

You may be able to reduce the number of bathrooms needed:
- Provide a wash-up sink at service entry.
- Install a lavatory in a bedroom or hallway closet, Fig 11-3.
- Use a compartmented bathroom, Figs 11-2f, 11-2j, and 11-2k.

Consider the following desirable features, too.
- A lavatory in a separate compartment from the tub/shower eliminates condensation on mirrors. Two or more can use the bathroom at the same time, Figs 11-2f, 11-2j, and 11-2k.
- An exhaust fan reduces odors and condensation on mirrors.
- Storage for towels, wash cloths, and soap near the tub/shower.
- Adequate towel racks within easy reach of bathers.
- A longer tub (5'-6" or 6') for tall people.
- Lavatories with large basins to reduce dripping water onto counters or floors.
- Swing-away faucets.
- Ground-fault-interrupt (GFI) convenience outlets above the bathroom counter for electric shaver, hair dryer, etc.

Special features to consider for a baby care area include:
- Single-bowl kitchen-type sink with swing-away faucet.
- Minimum 24" counter at the sink.
- Storage for baby clothes and supplies.
- Sliding cabinet doors so the baby cannot be injured by a swinging door above the counter.

Luxury considerations

This chapter shows minimum to moderate bathroom space allowances. You may want extra features such as:
- Direct access from a bathroom to an enclosed patio, deck, or pool for swimming, sunbathing, reading, or relaxing. Include space for supplies related to these activities, Fig 11-4.
- Whirlpool tub. Most of the many sizes require more space than a standard tub. Select your model before laying out bathroom space.
- Separate tub and shower, Figs 11-2c and 11-4.
- Sauna.
- Bench for sunlamp enjoyment, Fig 11-4.

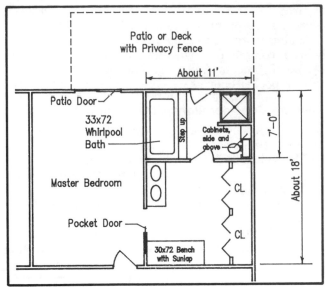

Fig 11-4. Master suite with luxury features.

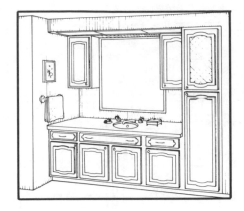

Safety
- Minimum 32″ door to admit wheelchair or person with walker.
- Grab bars for tub, shower, and toilet, Figs 11-5 and 11-6, securely anchored to house framing.
- Non-slip floor surfaces.

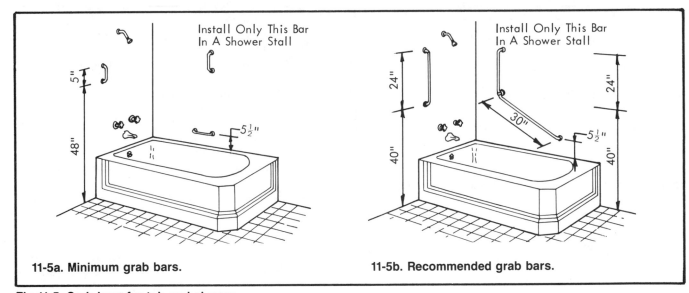

11-5a. Minimum grab bars. 11-5b. Recommended grab bars.

Fig 11-5. Grab bars for tub and shower.
A 12″ long grab bar on the front of the tub is often needed.

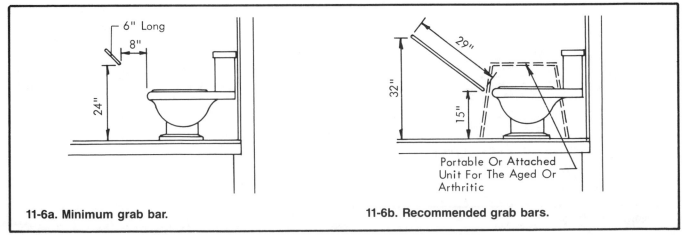

11-6a. Minimum grab bar. 11-6b. Recommended grab bars.

Fig 11-6. Grab bars on both sides of toilet.

12. BEDROOMS

Consider these factors when planning bedroom spaces:
- The number of sleeping rooms needed.
- Location of the rooms.
- Activities expected in each room, for the furniture and equipment needed, and to move around and dress comfortably.
- Personal needs of family members.
- Window and door placement.
- Closet space and location.

Number

Usually, no more than two people share a room. Separate bedrooms are often provided for:
- Parents or a single parent.
- Each child over 18.
- Each pair of same-sex children (age difference preferably no more than 4 years).
- Each pair of different-sex children if both are under 9 (age difference preferably no more than 4 years).
- Each additional adult or couple in the household.

Guests and family members from long distances often stay overnight. A separate guest room is ideal. However, a guest area can be in a multipurpose area such as the family room or study. A built-in bed, rollaway or couch, or sleeping bags, require little space.

Location

Locate bedrooms for privacy of sight and sound. Increase sound privacy with distance, sound-resistant construction and materials, sound-absorbing furnishings, finishes such as carpeting or acoustical ceiling tile, and barriers such as closets and baths. Achieve sight privacy by opening bedrooms off hallways rather than directly off another room.

Also consider how bedrooms relate to:
- One another (parents may like to be close to small children but separated from older ones).
- The bath (go from any bedroom to a bath without passing through another room).
- Work areas (particularly the kitchen and laundry).
- Social, recreation, and family spaces (to maintain quiet for sleep, study, and privacy, preferably without passing through the work area).
- Streets or major traffic areas (to minimize vehicle or pedestrian noises).
- Sun and breezes (see section on windows and doors).
- Supervising young children and caring for elderly or ill family members.
- Access by physically limited individuals.
- Conveniently handling soiled and clean clothing.

Fig 12-1 illustrates a variety of location options.

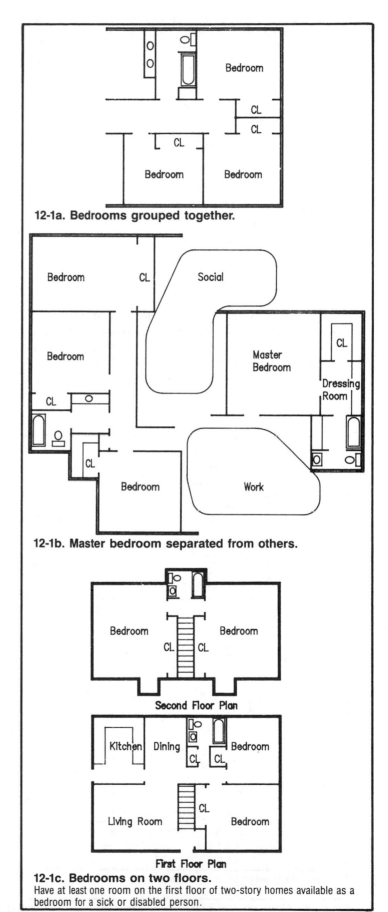

12-1a. Bedrooms grouped together.

12-1b. Master bedroom separated from others.

12-1c. Bedrooms on two floors.
Have at least one room on the first floor of two-story homes available as a bedroom for a sick or disabled person.

Fig 12-1. Typical bedroom locations.

Space Needs

Fig 12-2 shows minimum and optimum space for bedroom activities. The size of the bed is a major consideration. See Table 12-1. Fig 12-3 shows plans for various bed sizes and minimum and more desirable space allowances.

Bedrooms are often retreats for isolation and personal space for private and individual activities. To meet these needs, provide for the needed furniture, equipment, etc. Consider bunk beds or lofts to save floor space for other uses. See Fig 12-4.

Consider this partial list of bedroom uses:
• Study or office/work space (desk, chairs, lighting, bookshelves, and computer storage).
• Play space for young children (open area and storage).
• Private relaxation (comfortable chairs, tables, lighting).
• Storing recreation equipment (television, stereo, VCR, tape storage, etc.).

Space for these needs can significantly increase the cost of the home, so compromises are often necessary. However, if this space replaces or reduces needs elsewhere, costs can balance. As family members leave, bedrooms can be put to other uses.

12-2c. At closet.

12-2d. Dressing circle.

12-2a. Making a bed.
Twin bed can be made from one side, so bed can be only 4″ from wall.

12-2b. Between bed and dresser.
The minimum distance is with the person to the side of the pulled out drawer.

12-2e. Children and furniture height graph.

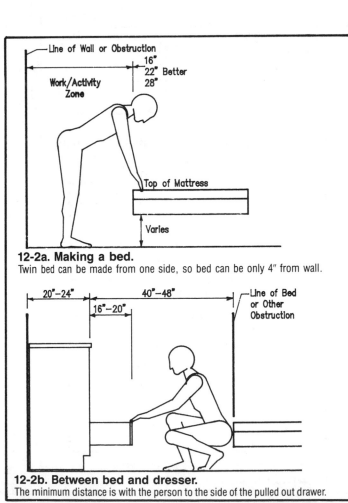

Fig 12-2. Minimum and optimum spaces for bedroom activities.
For person seated at desk or dresser, see Work Center Dimensions, Chapter 6.

Table 12-1. Typical bed dimensions.

Lengths include 3″ (1½″ each end) for metal or wooden headboards and footboards; add another 7″ length for bookcase-type headboard.

12-1a. Bed sizes.

Based on common mattresses; some other sizes are available.

Type	Width in.	Length in.
Standard crib	27	54
Standard	36	78
Twin	39	78
Full	54	78
Queen	60	83
King	78	83

12-1b. Waterbed sizes.

Width includes 3″ (1½″ per side) for the frame.

Type	Width in.	Length in.
Twin*	42	87
Super single	51	87
Full*	57	87
Queen	63	87
King	87	87

*Available, but less popular sizes.

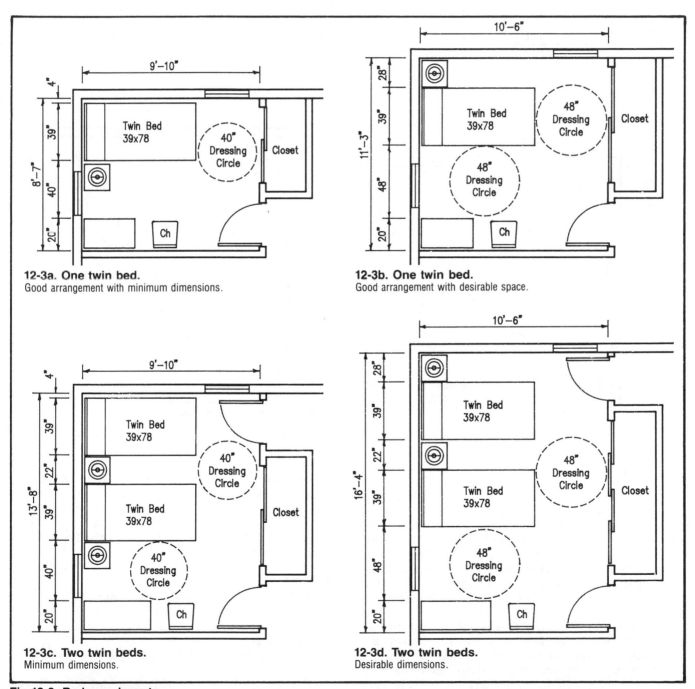

12-3a. One twin bed.
Good arrangement with minimum dimensions.

12-3b. One twin bed.
Good arrangement with desirable space.

12-3c. Two twin beds.
Minimum dimensions.

12-3d. Two twin beds.
Desirable dimensions.

Fig 12-3. Bedroom layouts.
Space is allowed only for sleeping and dressing.

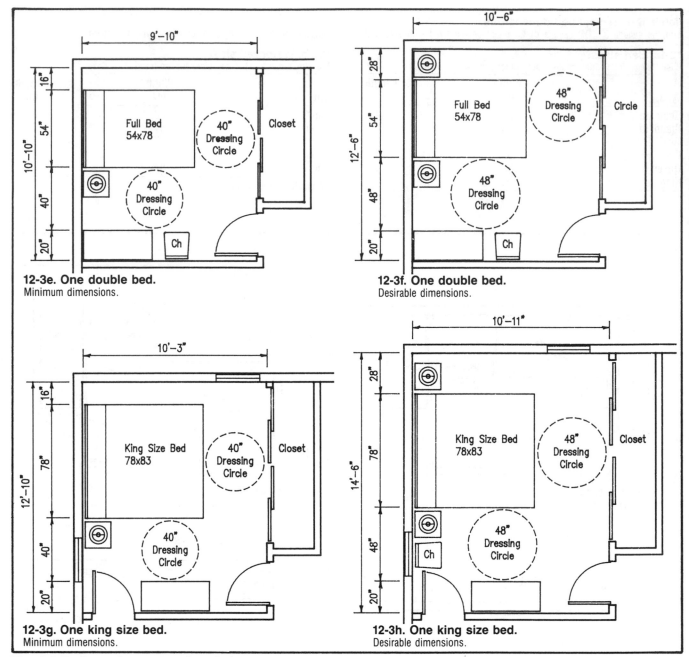

12-3e. One double bed.
Minimum dimensions.

12-3f. One double bed.
Desirable dimensions.

12-3g. One king size bed.
Minimum dimensions.

12-3h. One king size bed.
Desirable dimensions.

Fig 12-3. Bedroom layouts continued.

Window and Doors

Windows allow light, ventilation, and escape in case of fire. For these reasons, building codes usually dictate a minimum window area for bedrooms. Some codes require that at least one window in each bedroom be a potential fire escape. A 20″ wide by 24″ high opening is minimum. A sill 48″ off the floor may meet regulations but is too high for children. Window sills 16″-22″ above the floor allow bedridden persons to see out.

Window and door placements often dictate furniture arrangement. Low windows limit room arrangement and can limit changing the room's function in the future. High (strip) windows may increase both functionality and privacy but may give a boxed-in feeling. Check building codes to see if one low window is needed for a fire exit.

Windows in more than one wall allow cross ventilation. Doors across from a window also help air circulation throughout the house. Two windows together, rather than separated, in the same wall may provide more light and easier window treatments and furniture arrangements.

Closets

Put bedroom closets near the entry, Fig 12-5:
• To save time and energy, such as for mid-day clothes changes and for returning clean clothes to the room.
• To save space—more usable bedroom floor space often results.

A closet light is desirable, especially for closets that are deep or off poorly lighted areas. Automatic door switches are available.

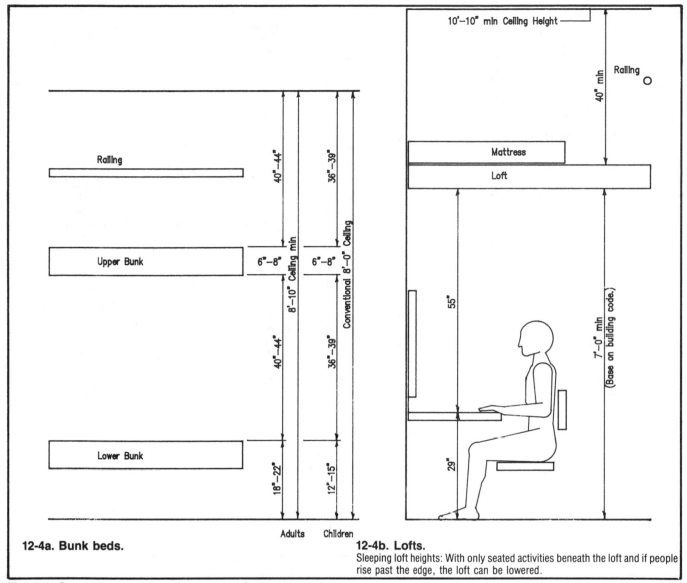

12-4a. Bunk beds.

12-4b. Lofts.
Sleeping loft heights: With only seated activities beneath the loft and if people rise past the edge, the loft can be lowered.

Fig 12-4. Space requirements for bunk beds and lofts.
Design lofts and select bunks to avoid head injury. Provide a safe ladder to upper bunk or loft.

Fig 12-6 shows closet types and space needed for garments to be accessible. Table 12-2 recommends closet dimensions.

Closet doors

Five closet door types are common, Fig 12-7. Consider cost, appearance, ease and safety of operation, wall space required, door projection or swing, and net opening size. Closet doors are usually 6'-8" (80") high.

A 1"-2" space under the door allows air circulation in the closet and helps reduce mildew in humid conditions. Louvered doors further improve circulation and might be needed where moisture condensation may be a problem, such as closets on outside walls, below grade, or where humidity is high.

Table 12-2. Clothes closet dimensions.
Provide at least 48" of rod space per person plus additional space for off-season storage.

	Clear interior dimensions, in.
Depth	24-28
Rod length, per person	48
Shelf depth	12-18
Rod height to center of pole:	
Street clothing	62
Woman's evening clothing	72
Double rods: upper	81
lower	40
Clothing for children 6-12	45
Distance between rod and shelf	2
Distance between closet hooks	7
Shelves above 76" are useful for seldom used items.	

12.6

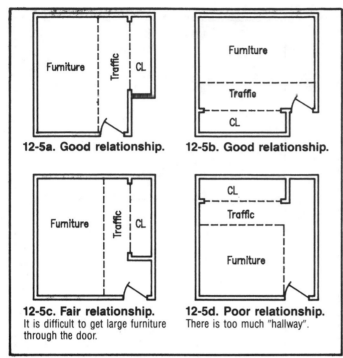

12-5a. Good relationship.   **12-5b. Good relationship.**

12-5c. Fair relationship.
It is difficult to get large furniture through the door.

12-5d. Poor relationship.
There is too much "hallway".

Fig 12-5. Bedroom door-closet relationships.

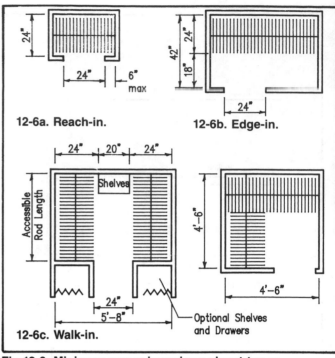

12-6a. Reach-in.   **12-6b. Edge-in.**

12-6c. Walk-in.   Optional Shelves and Drawers

Fig 12-6. Minimum space in various closet types.

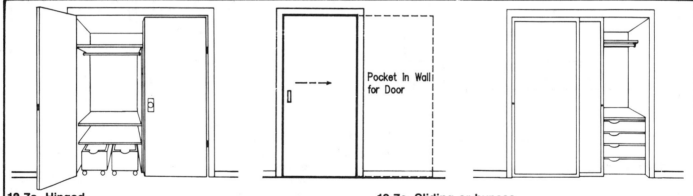

12-7a. Hinged.
Allow space for the door to swing. Doors are 24″-36″ wide and are single or in pairs. You can hang closet accessories on the inside face of the door. Fasten closet hardware to the side or top rails of a flush door with a hollow core.

12-7b. Sliding or pocket.
These do not block the closet opening or project into the room. Wall space must be available for the pocket. Avoid hanging heavy shelving, etc., on the walls along the pockets.

12-7c. Sliding or bypass.
These do not interfere with access space or passing traffic. But, the door blocks part of the opening, which is unhandy with narrow doorways.

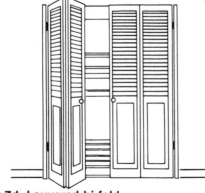

12-7d. Louvered bi-fold.
Two panels, 12″-18″ wide, make a bi-fold door. One or two bi-fold doors close openings to 72″ wide. The door panels project into the room less than hinged doors, so they need less clearance.

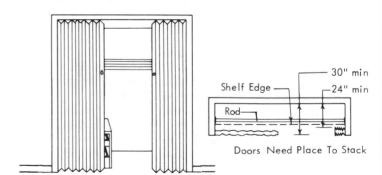

12-7e. Folding (accordion).
The full closet opening between the folded doors, is accessible. The doors are narrow strips of wood or vinyl-covered metal frames and are 25″ and wider.

Fig 12-7. Closet doors.

13. STORAGE

The need for adequate storage space cannot be over-emphasized, because it makes daily living easier by helping keep the household organized. Lack of good storage space is a common deficiency.

Keep items for daily activities easily accessible in what is called **live storage.** Provide adequate live storage and space for infrequently used or seasonal items. Holiday decorations, garden equipment, and lawn furniture can be less accessible.

Storage needs depend on the household's and each family member's lifestyle and needs. Recommendations vary from 10%-25% of the home's total floor area. Include the floor space of closets and kitchen cabinets in this estimate. The square footage recommendation helps decide length and depth, but also consider storage height.

Large items need special storage areas, perhaps with extra height. Examples include large suitcases, golf clubs or skis, and folding chairs.

Storage Principles

These guidelines help plan functional storage spaces.

1. Provide storage near where an item is needed first or most often:
   a. Match activities and rooms. Store items in or near that room.
   b. Store duplicates in more than one place to save steps, e.g. cleaning equipment and supplies in each bathroom.
   c. If used together, store together; e.g., keep cleaning equipment and supplies in one place.
2. Consider the length, height, and depth needed. See Table 13-1 for common depths. Provide flexibility (such as adjustable shelves) to meet changing needs.
3. Store frequently used items about 25"-59" off the floor for easy reach without bending or stretch-

Table 13-1. Range of depths for storing common items.

Item	Depth, in.	Item	Depth, in.
Appliances, small kitchen	6"-24"	Footware	10"-12"
Bakeware	12"-24"	Games and toys	12"-24"
Bath linens	12"-18"	Garden equip.	3"-36"
Bath supplies and equip.	4"-18"	Glassware	4"-12"
Bed, folding	12"-24"	Handicrafts	24"
Bedding	12"-24"	Holiday decorations	12"-48"
Beverages (6, 8, and 12 packs)	12"-16"	Infant's equip.	24"
Books	8"-16"	Kitchen utensils	4"-16"
Business papers	12"-16"	Luggage	24"
Card table	4"	Magazines	8"-12"
Cleaning equip.	18"-30"	Medicines	4"-6"
Cleaning supplies	4"-8"	Movie and slide projection equip.	20"-24"
Clothing		Musical instruments	12"-36"
In drawers	8"-16"	Radios	4"-12"
On hangers	24"	Record player, records	16"
On hooks	16"-20"	Serving dishes	12"-18"
Cookware	12"-24"	Sewing equip.	24"
Computer equip.		Sporting equip.	12"-28"
Monitor	24"	Stereo equip.	8"-24"
Keyboard	8"-12"	Table linens	16"-20"
Computer	—	Television	24"
Cutlery	9"-12"	Tools	
Dinnerware	4"-12"	Mostly hand-held	4"
Drawer files	16"	Power	12"-36"
Electric fans	12"-16"	Trays, platters, bowls	8"-16"
Folding chairs		Typewriter	
Narrow side out	18"-24"	Portable	16"
Broad side out	4"	Standard	20"
Food stored in:		Vacuum cleaner, tank type	24"
Bottles	4"-8"		
Canned foods	4"-8"		
Boxes broad side out	4"-8"		
Boxes narrow side out	8"-16"		
Staples	4"-12"		

ing. Put seldom used light items above, and heavy items below these levels.

4. Store items for:
   a. Visibility: one row deep, if possible, so they can be seen; items not seen are forgotten. Or store like items behind each other.
   b. Accessibility: for easy grasp, removal and return without affecting other items (particularly frequently used ones and emergency medicines).
   c. Protection from environmental damage: beware of heat, moisture, fumes, insects, and rodents in locations such as basements or attics.
   d. Safety: keep medicines, cleaners and other chemicals, guns and ammunition, and dangerous tools out of children's reach. Do not store cleaning supplies or medicines under a sink unless the cupboard is locked. Install a positive latch above young children's reach on cleaning closets and other hazardous storages. Select a fastener that is not self-latching to prevent a child being locked in.
   e. Keep old things with sentimental value, but discard never-used and out-dated items. Has it been used in the last year or so?

5. Finally, for each storage device, consider:
   a. Open or closed? Closed devices hide clutter and things not very attractive or appealing. Open ones, however, can display valuable possessions, collectibles, and decorative articles. Open storage devices do not protect from dust, grease, dirt, or light.
   b. Movable or built-in? Storage units that are portable or can be easily dismantled can be moved to a different room or house. A finished appearance on all sides and extra strength to make them self-supporting may cost more than built-ins.

   Built-ins are logical for households planning to stay in the home for some time. Utilizing space between wall studs adds storage and both visual and actual floor area; both factors increase comfort in homes downsized to increase affordability. Finally, built-ins may cost less by relying on the dwelling's structure, rather than the storage device, for strength. And, only the front of many built-ins must be finished, which can lower cost.

Storage Devices

Storage devices, Figs 13-1 to 13-8, are most useful if they are:
- Flexible, for changing needs; such as adjustable closet rods for longer clothing of growing children, adjustable shelves, pegboard, and adjustable or removable dividers.
- Capable of protecting and/or displaying stored items.
- Efficient, to use all available space and give just enough room to remove and replace items easily.

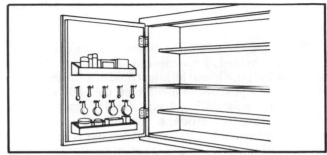
Fig 13-1. Hooks, pegs, and racks.

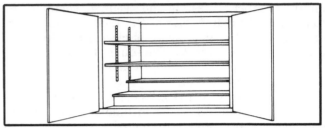
Fig 13-2. Shelves.

Fig 13-3. Soiled clothes storage.
Three sides are perforated board or plywood with ventilation holes.

Hooks, pegs, and **racks** can support heavy loads (bicycles) or light items that need to be grasped easily, such as belts, ties, shoes, or the spices and measuring spoons in the cabinet of Fig 13-1.

Shelves store all kinds of things. They may be fixed, adjustable, or pull-out, and can attach to or hang from walls, ceilings, etc. Variations include steps and half-shelves (about ½ the height and width of fixed ones) to increase surface space.

Boxes and bins store bulky items, such as soiled laundry or many food items. Dividers often make items more accessible.

Drawers are bins that pull out for convenience. Divide drawers, especially large ones, to improve usefulness.

Sliding trays are shelves with the convenience of drawers. If a storage is deeper than 20", trays can be closer together than fixed shelves with the same access to stored items. Pop-up trays are particularly useful for small kitchen appliances that must be accessible without being kept on the counter.

Storage furniture, such as chests and dressers, usually have shelves and drawers. They are freestanding or built-in and usually have a variety of storage space sizes.

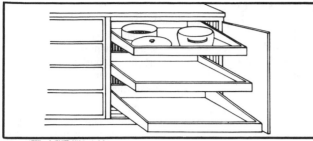

Fig 13-4. Sliding trays.
(Pull-out shelves.)

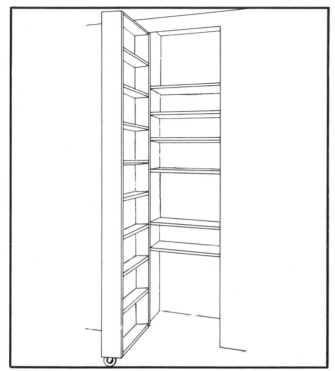

Fig 13-5. Storage door.

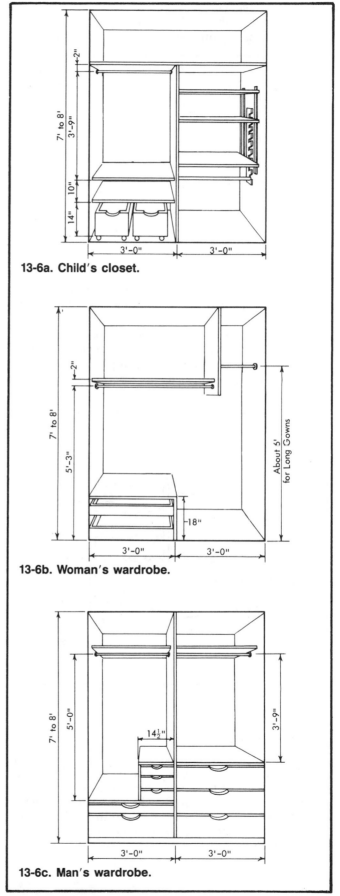

13-6a. Child's closet.

13-6b. Woman's wardrobe.

13-6c. Man's wardrobe.

Fig 13-6. Closets.

Cabinets provide storage near the floor (base cabinets), on walls (wall cabinets), or to full wall height (pantries or closed bookcases). Cabinets include shelves, drawers, boxes, bins, hooks, pegs, and racks to make them functional.

Store medicines away from humidity and heat sources or in the refrigerator, as recommended by the manufacturer. Prevent access by children—an unlocked bathroom cabinet may be a poor place.

Closets hold clothing, linens, and some seasonal items. They often have rods, pegs, racks, and shelves, but drawers and other storage devices can be added. A storage door with shelves, heavy hinges, and support wheel can neatly store canned goods or other items, Fig 13-5. Good design uses the space under shorter hanging garments and above the clothes rod. Closets can sometimes be converted to office or sewing space or a half-bath. See Fig 13-6.

Room dividers can be movable storages that also help separate living areas. Consider dividing large open plan spaces into more intimate areas: living room from guest entry, living room from dining room, dining area from kitchen, or sleeping from dressing or relaxation spaces in large bedrooms. A large room divider needs sub-dividers: shelves, drawers, cabinets, and bins to improve usefulness. See Fig 13-7.

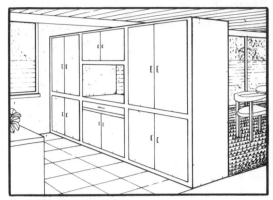

Fig 13-7. Room dividers.

Modular units have standard-sized components, usually based on 3″ or 4″ dimensions, that can be combined as desired. Components include: boxes, shelves, cabinets, drawers, desks, closets, etc. They can be stacked, hung, connected, or separate. Modular units are particularly appealing for remodeling or for expanding storage as needs emerge and resources permit. Fig 13-8.

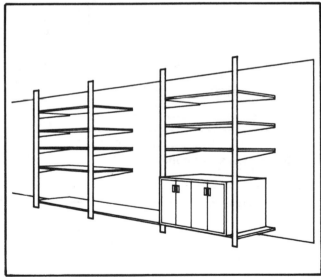

Fig 13-8. Modular units.

Grouping Similar Items

Some things need to be in specific rooms. Others can be put anywhere that is convenient, depending on room size, kind, number, and location. If the plan includes a hall, for example, cleaning supplies in this central area may serve better than in a utility room. The following lists suggest common groups and preferred storage location.

Kitchen storage
See the chapter on kitchens.

Usual
food (boxed, canned, fresh)
spices and condiments
staples
bakeware
cookware
dinnerware and flatware
cleaning supplies

kitchen linens
small appliances
articles supporting each
  work center
medicines

Possible
cleaning equipment and supplies
tools (hammer, screwdriver, etc.)

Utility room

Usual
laundry supplies
sewing supplies
foods (bulk, canned, frozen)
canning or freezing supplies
work and play clothes/coats
cleaning equipment, supplies
ironing board and equipment
house plant supplies
  and equipment

Possible
sports equipment
gardening supplies and small
  garden tools
out-of-season equipment
non-flammable paints
painting equipment

Avoid pesticides, herbicides,
  or flammables in the house.
Prevent access to them by
  children.

Cleaning closet

Usual
vacuum cleaner
mops
broom
dust pan
buckets
cleaning equipment
cleaning products
step stool

Possible
laundry supplies
window cleaning equipment

Bathroom
See the chapter on bathrooms.

Usual
bath linens
toilet supplies
cosmetics
cleaning supplies
personal care appliances
paper products

medicines

Possible
scale
soiled clothing, linen
bedding
exercise equipment

Living or family room

Usual
books
magazines
musical instruments
radio, stereo, tape deck
television
card tables
folding chairs
snack trays
wood for fireplace
fireplace/woodstove equipment
collectibles
projector, screen

Possible
coats
desk supplies
computer equipment and supplies
typewriter
business papers
toys
games
sports equipment
video equipment
exercise equipment
folding bed

Dining room

Usual
table linens
dinnerware
flatware
glassware
table leaves

Possible
sewing equipment
business papers
desk supplies
typewriter

Bedroom

Usual
clothing (hanging, folded)
bedding
cosmetics, jewelry
bedtime medicines
personal care products,
 appliances
accessories

Possible
soiled clothing
folding bed
desk supplies
typewriter
sewing equipment
radio, tv, stereo or tape deck
baby supplies
luggage
sports and hobby equipment
toys
exercise equipment

Hallway

Usual
coats, hats, overshoes
sports equipment
cleaning equipment
cleaning supplies
bedding
cold weather garments
umbrella

Possible
folding bed
card tables
folding chairs
luggage
dining table leaves
home movie or slide equipment

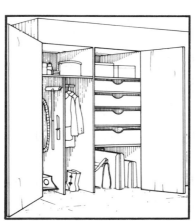

Study or den

Usual
books
magazines
desk supplies
typewriter
business papers
sewing equipment
computer equipment and supplies
office files

Possible
folding bed
clothing
musical instruments
radio, stereo or tape deck
card tables and folding chairs
sports and hobby equipment
toys
video equipment

Garage, basement, or attic

Usual
Christmas decorations
power tools
luggage
garden and lawn supplies
bikes/trikes
storm windows/doors and screens
paints and paint supplies
snow tires
window air conditioner
barbecue grill
outdoor furniture
baby carriage
home maintenance equipment
trunks
unused appliances, furniture
sleds/wagons
automotive equipment
sporting equipment

Possible
picnic supplies
camping equipment
sports equipment
lawn mower
garden hose
out-of-season clothing
canned goods

Extra Storage Space

Even after planning and allotting storage space for expected needs, households inevitably need extra storage for new or unexpected things. Ladders, bulky folding table and chairs, children's toys, or sporting equipment may have been forgotten or underestimated, for example. Some ideas for extra storage space follow. Also see MWPS-21, *Home and Yard Improvements Handbook,* listed in Chapter 20.

• Store folding table and chairs in a room divider.
• Recess a cabinet between interior wall studs for storage at the back of a counter. Sliding doors work well. Avoid electrical outlets and wires, which must be protected by wallboard or wood.

Recessed shelving increases noise transmission, unless there is a closet on the other side of the wall.
• Mount shelving over doors, or high on walls.
• Provide storage under built-in seating in a family room.
• Extend kitchen cupboards to the ceiling, or face soffits over cupboards with sliding doors.
• Install shallow shelves over a toilet tank.
• Utilize the space under beds or a loft, and over or under stairs.
• Provide suitable access to a dry crawl space.

14. MECHANICAL ROOMS AND BASEMENTS

Mechanical Rooms

Isolate the furnace and hot water heater from the rest of the house in a separate room or closet. With an unfinished basement, partitioning can be delayed. Leave room for servicing. Install a door wide enough to replace the equipment, usually off the central hall of a basementless house or from outside in a mild climate.

Consult local building officials for construction limitations, safety suggestions and requirements, and recommended space. Do not store flammable materials in the mechanical room. Separate the mechanical equipment from a laundry or workshop.

Locate the equipment near the center of the house, whether or not there is a basement, to avoid long runs of ducts and pipes. Insulate ducts and hot water lines to save heat and insulate cold water lines to reduce dripping due to condensation.

Basement Construction

In climates requiring deep frost footings, a full basement is relatively inexpensive. A basement under a single-story house adds 100% to the floor space but only 25%-50% to building costs.

A dry basement with south windows, insulation, and finished interior could be called the ground floor on a sloping lot. Lower levels can be as livable as the space above. Concrete and earth around a basement provide thermal heat storage at low cost, but do not substitute for insulation as a way of making comfortable space. Windows can provide light, ventilation, possible solar heat gain, and emergency exits.

Plan your basement for specific living spaces to meet current or anticipated needs. See the section on windows, and plan code compliance for future bedrooms and living areas, which is easier and less expensive during original construction. Include roughed-in plumbing and wiring for a possible bathroom.

Consider an unfinished ceiling higher than the usual 8'-0" (or fairly common 7'-4"). An 8'-8" or 9'-4" block wall allows for support beams, ducts, and other utilities above a standard 8' ceiling. Or gain extra ceiling height by running utilities through flat-chord floor trusses.

Suspended ceilings permit access to utilities for repairs or modifications. Insulate exterior walls during construction, even if the basement is not finished, to reduce heating and cooling costs and heating system size, and to reduce moisture condensation problems. Install insulation on the inside or outside of the wall.

For effective living space, a basement must be dry. Keep water away from the exterior walls, which is much easier and less expensive if done during construction. Give special attention to location, design, materials, and construction methods, Fig 14-1. Install roof gutters, drain tile around the footings, a sump pump, and damp proofing on the outer wall surfaces.

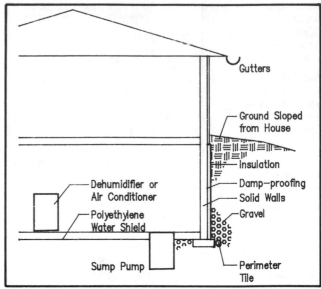

Fig 14-1. Dry basement features.
Select a high, dry site with well drained soil.

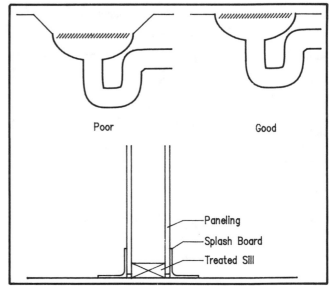

Fig 14-2. Drains.

Drains

Provide at least one floor drain. Slope floors gradually (1" in 8'-12') to a drain; recess the drain no more than ½" below floor level. Remember that any water that enters must be channeled around or under partitions to get to a drain. Make the lower portion of each partition moisture-resistant (preservative treated sills, rubber or plastic splash boards). See Fig 14-2.

Mechanical and Electrical Services.

Lower levels are ideal for locating water, sewer, telephone, electrical, cable television, and liquid and gaseous fuels services (which usually enter the house below ground).

Storm Shelter

Basements can provide a storm shelter. Increase protection by reinforcing the walls and ceiling in one corner of a basement room, preferably on the side from which storms come. The area can be finished living space and still serve in an emergency.

Stairway

A stairway near the service entry permits direct outside access to the basement. If the basement is primarily recreation or sleeping space, the stairway may start down from a central hall. In some large houses, multiple basement use may suggest two stairways.

Near a utility room on the first floor is a good location for stairs. On a farm, stairs with a landing may be just inside the service entry. You can enter the house and go directly to the basement or to the first floor, Fig 3-2.

Provide an unobstructed straight entry from outside to the basement, so bulky items can be handled without turning corners. A 36″ wide stairway is desirable; 40″ wide is better. Stairs may lead to the recreation room or a hallway.

Basement Rooms

A good arrangement has a lengthwise partition near the center of the basement, which supports the floor joists above. Rooms, hallways, and stairs are on either side of the supporting wall, Fig 14-3.

If ground slopes permit, a walk-out basement has good access and more light.

Bathroom with shower

Consider placing a bathroom under the first floor bathroom, kitchen, or utility room to simplify plumbing. Usually, a basement shower costs less than a tub. See the chapter on bathrooms.

Recreation room

With the supporting wall down the center, one side of the basement can be flexible and attractive recreation space with no supporting posts. Space for table tennis, pool, television viewing, and dancing is created. A minimum width is 12′, and more is better. Length depends on the activities planned.

Bedroom

Guests or family members often like the privacy of a separate floor for their bedroom, especially if a bathroom is provided. Provide the same privacy, size,

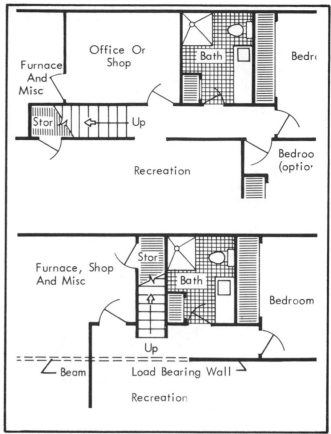

Fig 14-3. Basement layouts.
Possible space use in a basement.

and storage space as on the first floor. Check local building codes for possible limitations on basement living space. Take special care to provide light, a safe exit, and a dry location.

Other Activities

Basement space is usually more economical than first floor space. Other uses include hobby areas, shop, and storage of out-of-season, bulky, and seldom used items. Often the family finishes the basement as time and funds permit, providing both savings and enjoyment. Develop the basement plan along with the rest of the house regardless of when the finishing will be done.

Some families must build the basement first and live in it until time and funds permit completing the house. This practice is usually limited to rural areas.

15. GARAGES AND CARPORTS

A garage or carport shelters a car but can also be multiple-use space. Plan location and size to suit how you want to use the garage or carport.

Advantages of Garages and Carports

Either a garage or a carport can protect a car and passengers, reduce scraping frost from windows, and protect a car's finish. Either can also provide some storage space. In cold climates, a garage is usually preferred. An alternative is a one-car garage next to a one-car carport, as in Fig 15-1.

Garage uses:
- Help protect the house against winter wind and summer heat.
- Provide storage for garden equipment, outdoor furniture, bicycles, and bulk storage.
- Double as workshop.
- Provides space for utilities (furnace, water heater, washer and dryer).
- Provide bad-weather play area for children.

Carport uses:
- Provide low-cost garage space that does not completely block light or breeze.
- Double as outdoor living area.
- Provides year-round play area for children in mild climate.

Fig 15-1. Combination garage and carport.

Location

The garage or carport is usually near the service entry. The garage area can be the entry court to the house, with both guest and service doors accessible from the driveway. A turn-around area may be desirable, or even necessary with a long driveway or a busy street. Driver needs to be able to see that driveway is clear of people and obstructions.

The garage can sometimes protect the house from winter winds without blocking summer breezes, Fig 15-2. Avoid blocking a desirable view from social areas of the house.

Size

Decide on the number of vehicles to be housed. Consider campers, bicycles, motorcycles, lawn mowers, snow blowers, and golf carts. Allow for a shop, play space, storage, and other planned uses.

It costs more to build a single garage and enlarge it later, than to build a double garage. A small single garage that allows only for a car is seldom advisable. Sizes are shown in Fig 15-3. A minimum double garage is 20'x20', but a 24'x24' is recommended to allow for opening doors, moving around the car, and for some storage. Increase the size if more storage or work space is needed.

Use

Garage storage is on the side or back walls, suspended from the ceiling, or in a full attic or loft above the ceiling. See Fig 15-4. Closets, shelves, cabinets, hooks, and other storage devices are helpful. You may want to keep cabinets up off the floor for ease in cleaning.

A carport storage unit is shown in Fig 15-5. Fig 15-6 shows a storage opening from outside the garage for yard and garden equipment. Storage can be outside the wall, Fig 15-7. Heating a garage allows for play, shop, or laundry areas and for storing items that may freeze, such as paint.

Doors

Install 9' wide overhead doors in a new single garage, 16' wide in a double. Doors 8' wide are common in older garages. Two 9' doors side by side are also quite common. An electric door opener is convenient.

At least one walk-in door is recommended to avoid opening the big door or for access to a rear yard. Have doors blend with the style of the house. Attention drawn to a walk-in door may encourage visitors to use it instead of the guest entry. An overhead door may not meet code exit requirements.

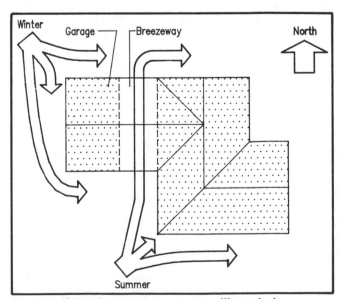

Fig 15-2. Orienting a garage to prevailing winds.
Winter protection without blocking summer breezes.

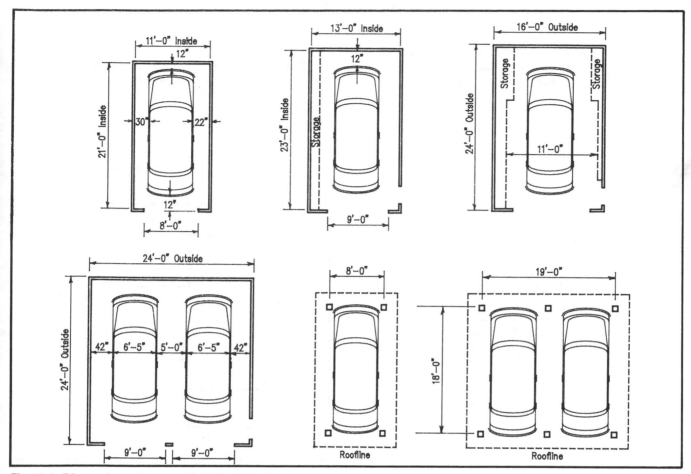

Fig 15-3. Dimensions for garages and carports.
Sizes are for full-size American sedans—about 6½'x19'. Consider a floor stop for the front wheels to protect the rear wall.

Fig 15-4. Attic or loft storage.

Fig 15-5. Carport storage unit.

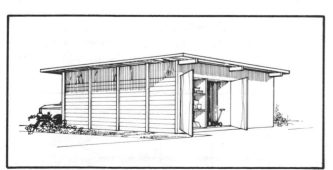

Fig 15-6. Garden equipment storage in back of garage opens to yard.

Fig 15-7. Storage outside the garage wall.

16. REMODELING

Remodeling is one way to improve older housing. But it requires many complex decisions about financing, materials, costs, plans, specifications, contracts, and codes. Reasons to remodel include:
- Moving is not feasible or desirable.
- Saving costs of ownership transfer to help pay for improvements.
- Saving a special, architecturally significant house.
- Wanting to improve a family homestead.
- Preserving structural soundness sometimes unmatched in new construction.
- Saving good exterior proportions and large rooms that can yield a satisfactory floor plan at less cost than new construction.
- Improving a house before selling.
- Remodeling in stages as money is available and while living in the house.

Reasons for not remodeling include:
- Finding that changing the house will not change the factors causing dissatisfaction (e.g., unsatisfactory neighborhood, inconvenient location, zoning regulation prohibiting desired additions, etc.).
- Unwillingness to undertake major changes with uncertain estimates of the cost and time required.
- Avoiding family stress and the dust, dirt, clutter, and inconvenience.
- Financing costs—home improvements are generally at higher interest rates than a home mortgage.
- High cost of improvements (e.g., wiring, plumbing, structural) that should not be attempted by inexperienced remodelers, even to save money.
- Avoiding the high cost of major structural or utility deficiencies, especially if the neighborhood has declined. It is sometimes impossible to recover improvement expenses through higher resale value.

If, after considering the pros and cons, you still consider remodeling your best housing alternative, develop a remodeling plan. Whether you are remodeling a single room or the entire house, develop an "as-is" plan of the entire house. If your remodeling includes an addition, you will also need a plot plan.

Developing the Remodeling Plan

Put ideas on paper to compare alternatives. It is difficult to stand in a livingroom and visualize dividing it into a bedroom, closet, and bathroom until you see it on paper. Make scale drawings that include wall thicknesses.

Preparing an "As-Is" House Plan

Have someone help you take measurements of the house. Get a 25' steel tape measure.

Draw the house layout on graph paper with 4 or 8 divisions to the inch. Use a scale of ¼" = 1'-0" (on a ruler, 1" = 4', ⅛" = 6", ⅟₁₆" = 3").

Exterior measurements
1. Begin at an outside corner. Measure from corner to corner, ignoring doors, windows, and porches.
2. Write the dimensions from corner to corner to the nearest full inch. Check total dimensions on opposite sides of the house against each other (they really may not be the same).
3. Add porches, steps, etc.
4. Draw a second line to show wall thickness, Fig 16-2.

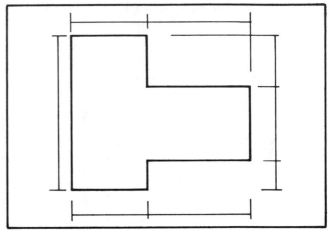

Fig 16-1. Basic plan outline.

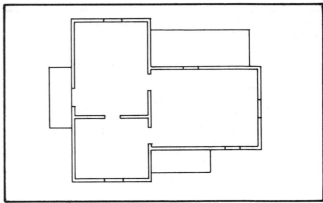

Fig 16-2. Wall thickness shown.

Interior measurements
1. Begin in one corner of a first-floor room. Measure to the nearest full inch from corner to window or door jamb, from jamb to jamb, and from jamb to the next corner (disregard window and door trim), Fig 16-3. Measure and record the overall width and length of the room, and check against the total of the dimensions along each interior wall.

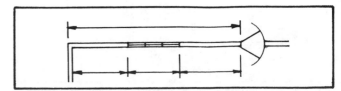

Fig 16-3. Measuring doors and windows.

2. Do the same for each room in the house. Use a tracing paper overlay for the second floor and the basement plans. Trace walls that carry through two floors, and measure only any additional walls.

3. Show stairways; count and record the number of steps. Label "up to second floor" or "down to basement" as shown in Fig 16-4.

4. For a new or revised stairway, measure the vertical distance from the first floor surface to the second floor surface and record it on the plan.

5. Measure the floor-to-ceiling height of each room and record it in the center of the room on your plan. If all rooms are the same height, record it only once, Fig 16-5.

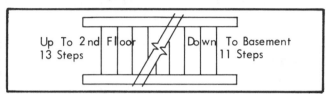

Fig 16-4. Stairway plan.

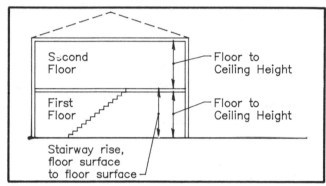

Fig 16-5. Vertical distances.

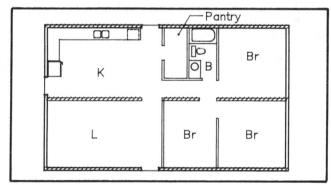

Fig 16-6. Bearing walls shown.
Kitchen and bathroom fixtures also shown.

6. Identify bearing walls by shading them or showing them in color, Fig 16-6. Bearing walls support joists or rafters. Sometimes the pattern of the lath can be seen through the plaster; ceiling joists are perpendicular to the lath.

7. Identify the rooms; show counters and fixtures in the kitchen and bathroom, Fig 16-6.

8. Show door-swing directions, types of windows, chimneys, and other features. Some suggested symbols are in Fig 16-7.

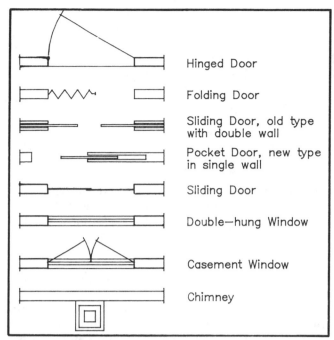

Fig 16-7. Drafting symbols for floor plans.

Preparing a Plot Plan

1. Draw the plot plan to scale. See Fig 2-1. For lots up to ½ acre, try a scale of 1" = 10'. Try 1" = 20' for larger sites where other buildings and landscape features need to be shown.

2. Start with a line near one edge of the paper to indicate the edge of the street or road. Then draw the driveway entry.

3. Draw the house plan relative to the driveway and the correct distance from the road. Locate items that could affect an addition: electrical service entrance, septic tank and disposal field, water service valves, etc. Investigate local zoning requirements for set-back, sideyard width, or other limitations on additions.

4. Locate major plantings (i.e., trees, large bushes, hedges) that must be avoided by an addition.

5. Locate outbuildings, concrete walls, slabs, and rock outcroppings.

6. Designate:
   a. True north.
   b. Prevailing winds by season.
   c. Prevailing odors (from farms, factories, and auto exhausts).
   d. Prevalent noises (from schools, roads, and factories).
   e. Desirable and undesirable views.

Preliminary Planning

List what you hope to accomplish, such as combination kitchen-dining or family-living room, three bedrooms, new utility room or bathroom, etc. The list will help you keep your goals in mind.

After the "as-is" plan is drawn to scale and you know what you want, you are ready to try a remodeling plan. Place transparent paper over the "as-is"

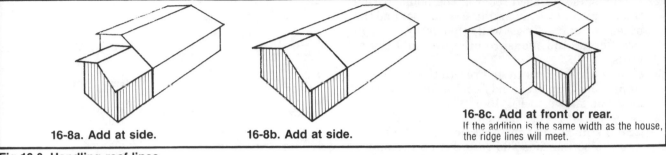

16-8a. Add at side.

16-8b. Add at side.

16-8c. Add at front or rear.
If the addition is the same width as the house, the ridge lines will meet.

Fig 16-8. Handling roof lines.

plan to draw the remodeling plan. Never draw new lines on the "as-is" plan. It is too valuable to mutilate or destroy. You will make many remodeling attempts, so keep the "as-is" plan as a reference for the starting point.

As you draw remodeling plans, use the criteria for designing a new house. Some compromises may be necessary.

Exhaust every possible idea for a good plan using available space before planning to add new space to an existing house. Consider developing an upstairs, unfinished attic, or basement.

If an addition is necessary, making it blend with the existing house is a challenge. Usually it is best to follow an existing roof shape and match the roofing and siding. Fig 16-8 suggests how to handle roof lines.

Try to make your remodeled house comfortable, convenient, and adequate for your family. Avoid trying to make a new house. Usually, you must tolerate some unlevel floors, perhaps a high ceiling (consider suspended ceiling), and some style features not found in a new house.

Remodeling Examples

Two "before" and "after" examples follow.

Example 16-1:
Situation
- Small rectangular house on narrow city lot, typical of thousands of prefabricated post World War II homes. See Fig 16-9.
- Concrete floors limit plumbing changes.
- Addition possible only to rear.
- Family must live in house during remodeling.

Desired changes
- New living room, kitchen, half-bath, and closet.
- Partition off utility room.
- Add patio and landscaping.

Procedure
- Add new living room to rear of house and finish completely.
- Convert old living room to new kitchen, tying in plumbing at back of washer-dryer.
- Build new half-bath and closet and enlarge existing bath. Minimum cutting of concrete floor to install plumbing.
- Partition off utility room.
- Add patio and landscaping.

Results
- Added space is less than ⅓ original area and probably will not be overbuilding for the neighborhood.

- Substantially more storage space.
- Good traffic pattern.
- Kitchen separated from living room by 12' long hall, which is a compromise to minimize plumbing changes in a concrete slab house.

Example 16-2:
Situation
- Two-story farm house with no first floor bath. See Fig 16-10.
- Seldom used front door.
- Congested back door area.
- Undesirable traffic through kitchen.
- No garage.
- Family can make temporary arrangements while kitchen is changed.

Desired changes
- Bathroom on first floor.
- Garage
- Upgrade windows.
- Improve traffic flow, especially in kitchen and at entrances.
- Improve kitchen.
- More open living and dining rooms.
- Office with access without going through rest of house.

Procedure
- Build the addition.
- Change stairway direction to give kitchen more wall space and to remove traffic from kitchen.
- Add second set of steps to back hall leading to new bath.
- Replace kitchen windows.
- Install new kitchen cabinets and appliances.
- Convert den into first floor bathroom and closets.
- Build garage.
- Install new floor covering in new and remodeled space.

Results
- New guest entry with coat closet, with access from farmstead's usual parking area.
- Office is located for easy access through the service entry.
- First floor bathroom accessible from service area and from living room.
- New efficient kitchen with eating space and no through traffic.
- Much more storage.

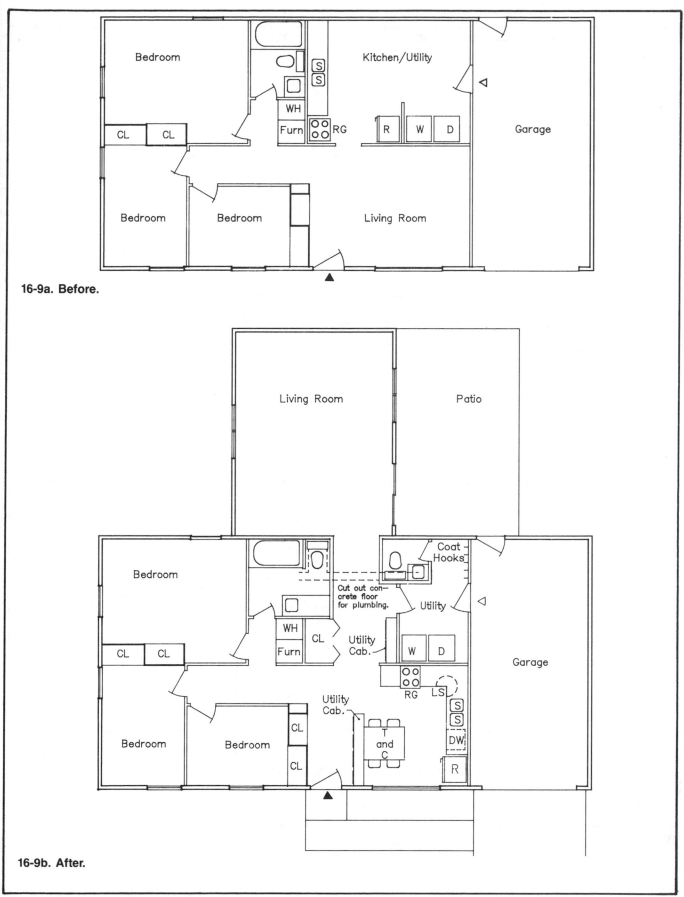

16-9a. Before.

16-9b. After.

Fig 16-9. Remodeling Example 16-1.

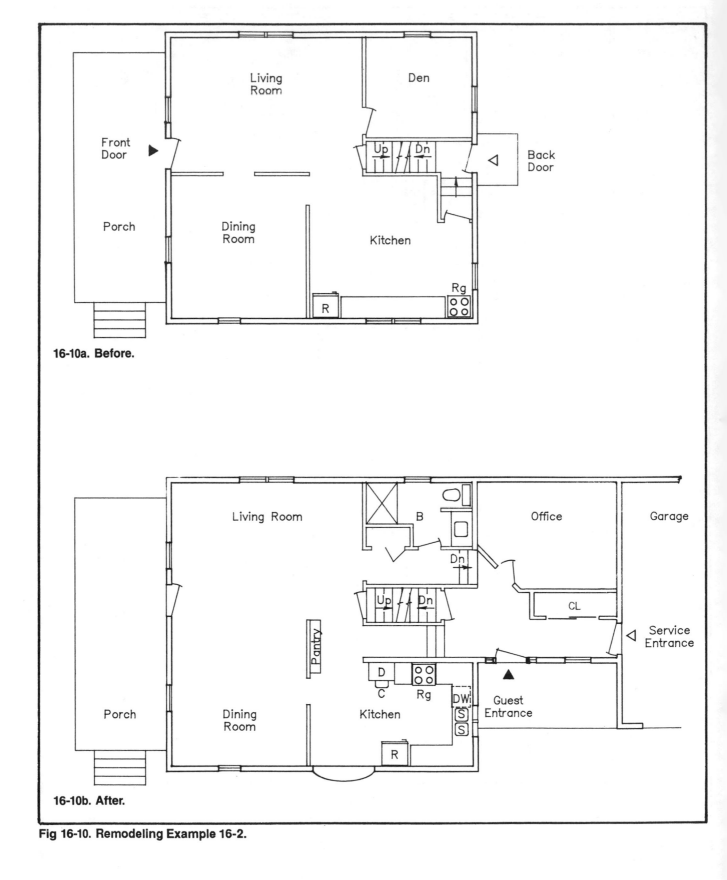

16-10a. Before.

16-10b. After.

Fig 16-10. Remodeling Example 16-2.

17. OTHER FACTORS AFFECTING SPACE USE

Construction Techniques

Fabrication

Housing units are fabricated in different ways. Good and poor quality can result from any method. This section acquaints you with some of the construction techniques you may choose from and the effect they can have on the floor plan.

- **Site built.** Materials are brought to the site for cutting and assembly. Any floor plan is possible.
- **Pre-cut.** Materials are cut and labeled in a factory, and are shipped to the site for assembly. The companies have stock plans, which the buyer can modify to some extent.
- **Panelized (pre-fab).** Floor, wall, ceiling, and roof panels are factory built and shipped to the site. Some entire homes are pre-fab. Modifications to stock plans usually are not possible.
- **Modular.** Modules (such as a bathroom) including floor, ceiling, and walls, are factory built. Site-built, pre-cut, or panelized houses can contain one or more modules, or an entire house can be assembled from modules. There may be some flexibility in combining modules into a floor plan.
- **Mobile.** The home is entirely built in a factory and towed to the site. Pick a model with good space planning. Single-wide mobile homes are 12'-14' wide and are usually parked on a slab. Double-wides are 24'-28' with two factory-built sections joined at the site, usually on a permanent foundation.

Energy Related Techniques

Many design and construction details that drastically reduce energy costs are relatively inexpensive. The savings in energy bills are often larger than any increase in mortgage. Energy efficient construction, efficient appliances, and least-cost energy sources can cut energy expenses by ⅔. Space and floor plans are affected by some techniques.

Solar orientation

Solar oriented houses have the long axis of the house east and west; most windows and the daytime living areas face south. The roof overhang exposes the glass to winter sun and shades the glass in summer, Fig 17-1. Solar orientation is affected by site and orientation of the house. Correct solar orientation reduces both heating and cooling bills. It also allows larger window areas for more daylight and better views.

Windows

Window location, size, and construction affect energy use, day lighting, interior comfort, privacy, views to the exterior, floor plan, furniture arrangement, interior decorating, fire exits, and appearance of the house.

Window types are in Figs 18-2 and 18-3. Provide at least storm sashes or double-glazing. For more energy efficiency, consider triple- or quadruple glazing, or double-glazing plus energy-saving coatings (low E). Select windows that meet federal and industry standards for air and water tightness.

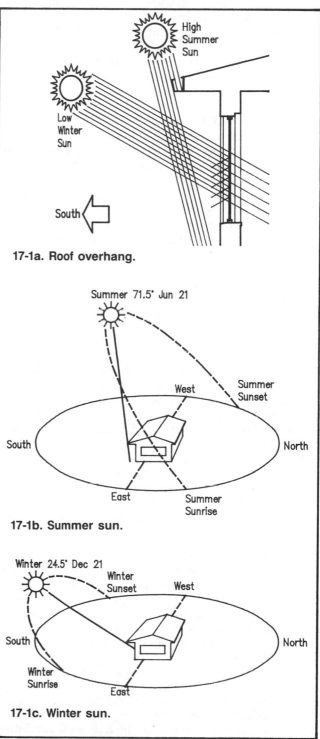

17-1a. Roof overhang.

17-1b. Summer sun.

17-1c. Winter sun.

Fig 17-1. Solar orientation.

To get desirable day lighting, south-facing windows are best for energy efficiency and interior comfort. With proper overhangs, they are cooler in summer and warmer in winter than other orientations. Draperies reduce nighttime heat loss. Well designed houses can have large amounts of south-facing glass.

North windows allow cross-ventilation and give pleasant, non-glare light. Select a small number of minimum size north windows with high R-values to reduce winter heat loss.

East and west windows, either for view or to capture morning or afternoon sun, are acceptable, but minimize size to reduce winter heat loss and summer heat gain. West windows are especially difficult: winter winds increase heat loss drastically, and summer sun heat gain is difficult to control.

Horizontal or sloped windows in the ceiling (skylights) have excessive summer heat gain and winter heat loss. Careful design can reduce these problems. Skylights offer privacy, light, and a view of the sky, but some are prone to breakage, water leakage, or condensation. Consider skylights carefully and in general, use sparingly.

Purchase only high-quality, tight-fitting windows. Casement windows are tightest. New weatherstripping materials make double-hung and sliding windows acceptably tight. Select window frames built to reduce heat flow. Steel and aluminum frames require a "thermal break".

Window glazing should be at least R 1.5, with 2.5 or more preferred for less heat flow. R-values of 5 and greater are available. (R-values measure resistance to heat flow. Larger Rs mean better insulation.) Reduced heat flow tempers interior glass surface temperatures, so rooms are more comfortable and winter moisture condensation is less. Higher R-values result from more layers of glazing (add storm windows or plastic film), wider air spaces between glazing, filling the air space with gas, and coating the glass with low-E material. Choose windows with at least two layers of glazing.

Obtain summer and winter performance data for all windows. For winter solar gain, select high R-values and high transmission of solar energy. Some windows with high R-values significantly reduce heat from sunlight and are unsuitable for windows intended to collect solar heat.

Passive solar systems

Most new solar houses now use passive, rather than active, solar systems. In a passive system, solar energy flows naturally, although some have small fans to assist air movement. The collector is usually south-facing glass or plastic. South-facing vertical windows work well for collecting solar heat and are less expensive, more readily available, and require less maintenance than solar collectors.

Orient the house to the south, and have it fully exposed to winter sun. Do not obstruct the sun with trees, buildings, etc. Sun energy is quite diffuse (weak) so make passive solar houses well insulated and tight.

Thermal mass stores heat: brick, concrete, water, and to some extent, gypsum wallboard. The mass reduces overheating on sunny winter days by storing heat for periods when the sun does not shine. Normal construction techniques store enough heat if the south window area is small. As the amount of south window area increases, more heat storage is needed. In general, the more heat storage provided, the more satisfactory the solar system.

Three types of passive solar heating systems adapt well for housing: direct gain, thermal storage wall, and sunspace, Fig 17-2. Solar houses often combine two or all three systems.

- **Direct gain.** Solar radiation passes through the south glazing directly into the living space. Heat storage is often concrete or brick floors. During the day, storage absorbs much of the incoming solar heat; at night, heat radiates from the stor-

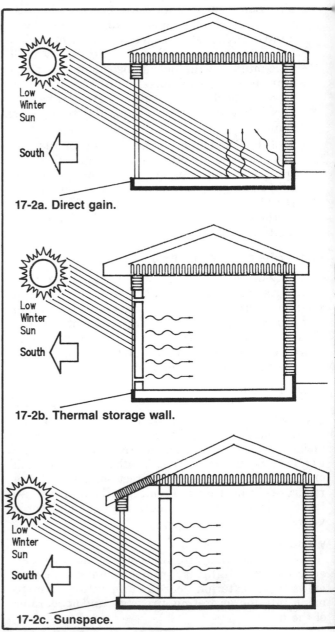

17-2a. Direct gain.

17-2b. Thermal storage wall.

17-2c. Sunspace.

Fig 17-2. Passive solar heating.

age to the living space. Direct gain systems suit living spaces with a good south view. Direct sunlight can produce glare and can fade many fabrics, so careful home design is needed. Glass that nearly eliminates fading is now available.

- **Thermal storage wall.** A large, heat storage wall (Trombe wall) is just behind the glass and looks like any other wall from inside the room. The wall may be concrete or stone 12"-16" thick or water 6" thick in drums, fiberglass tubes, or other containers. Paint the south side of the wall either a dark color to absorb solar energy or with a special low-E coating. The wall stores heat for release to the living space. Openings can be at the bottom and top of the wall to allow room air to pass between the wall and the glazing. This air warms before returning to the room. Rooms with Trombe walls warm slowly during the day and stay warm most of a night. Because they block the view, they are suited for rooms needing privacy, such as bedrooms. Windows can be placed in the wall if desired.
- **Sunspace.** A thermal storage wall is some distance back from the glass, instead of a few inches away. The sunspace between the glass and the wall may serve as an atrium, sunroom, etc. Massive floors, walls, benches, rockbeds, and covered pools of water can add heat storage. The sunspace usually fluctuates more in temperature than other house areas. To maximize winter heat collection and minimize summer overheating, avoid overhead glazing and insulate the ceiling well. Minimize east and west glazing. A large south-glazing area is needed for enough heat for the rest of the house. Sunspaces are not good greenhouses: most plants require more east, west, and overhead sunlight than in a heat collection sunspace and cannot tolerate the temperature extremes. Compromise designs combining sunspaces and greenhouses are possible, but they are not as energy-efficient as a sunspace alone.

Active solar systems

Fans and pumps move heat energy in "active" systems. They usually have a roof or wall mounted collector connected to a heat storage and distribution system. Solar orientation of the house is not essential, because the collector can be mounted and tilted to face south. Active systems are expensive and usually not cost-effective for house heating. They are most economical for heating domestic water, where the system works year round and performs very well in the summer.

Insulation levels

Insulating the house remains an important comfort and energy related technique. Adequately insulate the entire heated area of the house. Missed areas lose heat and might allow condensation and structural damage. The minimum insulation levels are (a large R is more energy efficient):

Ceiling	R-30
Walls	R-19
Floors over unheated areas	R-19
Foundations below grade	R-11

Construction techniques for enough insulation include:

- Superinsulated houses use much less heating and cooling energy because they have much more than minimum insulation levels. The high values often require attic truss changes, wider wall frames, and more foundation insulation. An adequate vapor barrier is required.
- Redesigned attic trusses permit extra thick insulation at the outer edges of the attic. In addition to less heat flow and more comfort, extra insulation near the sidewalls reduces or eliminates winter moisture condensation on the ceiling.
- Wider wall frames, with 2x6 lumber and rigid insulation beneath the siding and/or beneath the wallboard, reduce energy flows through the wall. R-values are typically R-24 or greater.
- Staggered double 2x4 stud walls have a large cavity (8" or more) filled with insulation and nearly eliminate direct conduction heat loss through the framing members. R-values are 25 and up, depending on wall thickness.
- Prefabricated wall panels and other construction methods are available to reduce heat flow through walls. R-values are 20 and up.
- Foundation insulation reduces heat loss and increases comfort. Use it for basements, crawl spaces, and concrete slabs. Insulate on the interior; or insulate on the exterior with rigid insulation protected from rodent and physical damage. The exterior method is easiest during construction, when the foundation is exposed. It does not take floor space from the interior and allows foundation walls to store heat. Protect insulation with a rigid material such as fiberglass, stucco, or mineral cement board to at least 2' below grade. Or, use insulated concrete sandwich construction.

  For an existing house, insulating the interior side is usually less expensive. Construct a wood stud frame inside the foundation and fill the stud cavity with fiberglass blanket insulation. Finish the wall with wallboard.
- Permanent wood foundations have wall cavities that can be easily insulated; install conventional interior finish.

Air exchange

Air leaks in new houses account for up to 50% of the energy loss. Also, moisture escapes through the leaks into attics and walls where condensation and freezing cause paint peeling and wood rot. Mold and mildew growth may cause health problems of occupants. Houses with more air leaks have higher energy bills and less controlled air-quality than tighter ones. Control is not possible in houses depending on leaks for ventilation. Over-ventilation wastes energy and removes too much moisture; under-ventilation allows pollutant and moisture build-up.

In new construction, prevent air and moisture from leaking with continuous vapor retarders and air barriers on the warm side of the insulation. Seal all holes into the attic around vents, plumbing stacks, attic access doors, chimneys, and wiring. Seal around electrical boxes and cracks where building materials meet, such as between the sill plate and the foundation.

Designers, suppliers, and contractors can help you select sealing techniques to make your house as tight as practical. Consider ventilating the house with mechanical (fan) ventilation. A heat exchanger for ventilation air reduces heat loss.

A house with few air leaks may not have enough natural ventilation to remove pollutants and moisture from living areas. Pollutants such as cigarette smoke, cooking odors, and out-gassing of composite and insulation materials can linger a long time in a tight house, causing irritation and health risks. Moisture comes from cooking, bathing, cleaning, laundry, plants, aquariums, etc., and can also cause problems.

In winter, excess moisture can condense and freeze on windows and in leaky walls. In summer, humidity can become uncomfortable. Mold and mildew can occur and structural rot is possible.

Exhaust ventilation near the source is often best. For example, exhaust fans in the bathroom and kitchen remove moisture and odors. Tight houses may require continuously running fans, often with ducts to individual rooms. Heat exchangers conserve energy. Supply fresh air intakes for fossil fuel and wood burning furnaces.

Attic ventilation

Attic ventilation removes moisture and heat and is separate from living area ventilation. Provide for air to enter the attic from the outside, typically through vents installed in the soffits. Also provide for air to leave the attic, typically through gable-end louvers or ridge vents. Gable-end louvers can be the inlets if adequate ridge vents are installed. Because vents retard air flow (with screens, deflectors, louvers, etc.), allow 1 ft² of free air inlet and 1 ft² of outlet for each 300 ft² of floor area. Commercial vents usually are rated for their net free area.

Efficient appliances

Efficient appliances often cut in half the energy consumed by inefficient units, but you probably cannot justify replacing working appliances. Refrigerators and freezers have been improved. Base purchases on estimated yearly operating costs, which are usually posted on new appliances.

Heating system

Some new heating systems are much more efficient than old ones. Electric, fossil fuel, and wood-burning equipment all have had major technical improvements. Typical chimneys are sources of high heat loss. New chimney dampers conserve energy.

New gas fired furnaces and water heaters have small pipes for air supply and exhaust, but no chimney. The pipes may be installed through the wall or the roof.

Resistance electric heating is about 100% efficient and usually the least expensive to install, but can be expensive to operate where electricity is relatively expensive.

Air-to-air heat pumps cost less to operate than resistance electric units and furnish air conditioning. Efficiencies have been steadily increasing, so compare efficiencies before purchase. Installed cost is higher than for resistance electric. To take advantage of off-peak electric rates, some utilities promote combining an electric heat pump with a fossil fuel furnace; heat storage can also help.

Water-source heat pump operating costs are comparable to those of high efficiency fossil fuel furnaces. Efficiencies vary, so ask for an estimate of yearly operating costs. Water-source heat pumps cost more to install, so carefully compare purchase price and operating costs over the life of the system.

Old design furnaces burning natural gas, LPG, or fuel oil had efficiencies of 60%-70% and are still available at a lower price. The newest systems are up to 97% efficient. Compare operating costs over the life of the furnace. In general, fuel savings justify buying higher efficiency units. High efficiency units control combustion air. Many have direct venting to the outside. Sealed combustion chambers eliminate the need for room combustion air, cannot back draft, and have safety and air quality advantages.

Open, wood-burning masonry fireplaces in exterior walls are not energy efficient, require large amounts of combustion air from the room, and are difficult to insulate. Some fireplaces actually lose more heat in the flue gases and lost room air than they produce.

Some wood-burning units are 80% efficient. They have tight fitting doors, controlled draft, blowers, combustion air ducting, tight fitting dampers, catalytic converters, and are located on inside walls. In tight new houses, install only high efficiency units with combustion air provided. Energy-efficient masonry units in the interior of the house have significant thermal heat storage mass, if insulation isolates the exterior chimney from the interior masonry. Wood-burning furnaces can be the primary or a supplemental heating system. To reduce fire risk, use approved heating units and chimneys installed by experienced professionals.

Air conditioners

Air conditioner efficiency has steadily increased. High efficiency lowers electric demand and operating costs. Extended heavy air conditioning needs can often justify the cost of high efficiency units.

Water heater

Thick, low-conductivity insulation reduces water heater tank losses; the extra cost is usually recovered in a year. Electric water heaters do not require combustion air.

Point-of-use instantaneous water heaters have no storage tank or stand-by losses but usually place a high demand on the energy source.

Water use

Water saving faucets and shower heads reduce energy and water costs. New design shower heads are satisfactory at ⅓ the water use of a more powerful shower head. Clothes and dishwashers with water conserving cycles reduce both water and energy use. Water conserving toilets, using 3 gallons or less per flush reduce cold water use.

Lights and other appliances

Fluorescent lights produce more light with less electricity than incandescent bulbs and have lower replacement cost. Use fluorescent or other high efficiency lights where suitable. Consider higher initial cost, light quality, and appearance of bulbs and fixtures.

Earth integrated

Earth integrated houses (earth-sheltered, -bermed, or -house) moderate temperature extremes with soil thermal mass to reduce energy for heating and cooling. Most earth houses do not drop below freezing even when utilities fail. The partial or full earth cover gives storm protection. Earth reduces air leaks, so most earth houses are tighter than conventional ones and usually require mechanical ventilation. They also require competent professional design and construction practices to resist high structural loads and to handle drainage, insulation, waterproofing, soil loads, and economics. The extra cost may outweigh advantages. The need for storage, natural light, and fire escape affects space planning.

Utilities

Appliances and utilities occupy space and affect space use. For example, placing the water meter and water heater in one corner and the gas meter and furnace diagonally across the basement in another corner may prevent developing living space in either end of the basement. The following general points may help you avoid similar problems and avoid potential problems. Check local codes for all utilities.

Basement House

- Cluster water, heating fuel, and electrical service entrances.
- Locate heating and cooling systems and water heater near the point of use, but not in a main room. Centrally locate heating and cooling systems for more uniform performance. Run ductwork for warm air heating parallel to main supports when possible.
- Avoid exposing plumbing lines from the first floor in basement living space.
- See basements use in Chapter 14.

Crawl Space or Concrete Slab House

In warm climates, the water meter, water heater, and furnace can be in the garage if permitted by local code and if precautions are taken to keep water from freezing. Seal and insulate furnace ducts.
- The furnace and water heater require at least 3'x6' floor space in a garage or closet inside the house. Check building codes and manufacturer's requirements for specific space, safety, and combustion air requirements. Provide clearance around the units for both fire safety and access for maintenance or replacement.
- In mild climates, heating systems are sometimes in attics. Provide access to the unit for maintenance.
- Put electrical service entrance in a utility room rather than a kitchen or bedroom.

Planning Space for Utilities

Meet codes that apply—contact local officials. Provide as generously as you can for present and future needs.

Electrical

- Provide convenience outlets on every wall and no more than 12' apart. More outlets help avoid extension cords and make it easier to arrange furniture. A 20 amp circuit can have up to 10 duplex outlets.
- Provide a light switch at every entrance to a room and at the top and bottom of stairs.
- Protect outlets with ground-fault interruptors (GFI) in the following areas: bathrooms, garages, kitchens if within 6' of a sink or countertop, outdoors if within 6'-6" of the ground, and at least one location in the basement. Also protect outlets near pools and fountains, hot tubs, etc. Install GFI outlets at the patio or deck, near the driveway or car service area, and near the front door. Check electrical codes.
- Consider outside flood lights.
- The kitchen and office need more outlets than other rooms. See the discussion of offices.
- In the kitchen, provide separate outlets for the microwave, dishwasher, and garbage disposal. Install outlets above the counter backsplash, alternating adjacent outlets between the two circuits. Space outlets close enough for 24" appliance cords. Limiting each kitchen circuit to less than the 10 outlet maximum is desirable.
- Provide adequate electrical capacity for future electrical loads, such as air conditioning and dishwashers. It is less expensive to provide extra capacity than to add it later.
- Consider telephone, television, and stereo locations and provide connections for them.
- A dedicated circuit with surge control is preferred, and often required for a computer.

Water and sewage

Before purchasing an urban lot, determine water and sewage location and elevation. Sanitary and storm sewers above the proposed basement floor level will prevent basement development or require costly lift pumps.

In rural locations, water supply and sewage disposal can be very costly. Determine the type of well needed for a safe water supply. Before construction, check the requirements for sewage disposal, including soil type, lot size, and ground slopes. Sewage disposal systems do not work properly in some soils.

- Plan at least two exterior hose bibs for lawn watering or car washing.
- Consider separate water heaters if you have widely separated needs or to supply 140° water for dishwashing.
- If you have your own well, space may be needed for a water pump, pressure tank, and perhaps a water softener.
- Locate the septic system far enough from the house to allow house expansion.
- Locate the septic tank for easy pumping and consider its affect on landscaping and outdoor living.

Heating and air conditioning
- Provide space for fuel storage—wood pile, propane tank, or oil tank. Consider affect of fuel storage on landscape planning and outdoor living.
- If wood is burned, store only a one-day supply in the garage or near the wood stove or furnace. Large amounts of damp wood in the house can cause moisture and insect problems.
- Place the air conditioning unit where its noise and heat will not affect outdoor living for you and your neighbors.
- Put the exhaust from a pulse combustion furnace where the noise can be dissipated or muffled, usually through the roof.
- Supply combustion air to fossil-fuel fired furnaces, water heaters, and wood-burners with a duct to the outdoors. Exception: If the appliance has a sealed combustion chamber it has its own vent to the outdoors. Electric units do not need combustion air.
- Consider the locations of heating and cooling ducts and registers. Ducts in the basement can interfere with remodeling. When possible, run the main duct parallel to support beams and individual ducts between the floor joists. Floor trusses provide spaces for underfloor ducts. Put heat registers and radiators at outside walls near greatest heat loss, typically under windows. Avoid blocking registers and radiators with furniture or draperies.
- Radiant heat (hot water heat in the floor or radiant electric ceiling panels) requires no floor area and allows complete freedom in furniture arrangements.
- Ceiling air-conditioning outlets work well and allow flexibility in furniture arrangement. Attic ducts must be carefully sealed and insulated.

18. EXTERIOR HOUSING STYLES

The National Association of Realtors (NAR) recognizes 58 different American house styles. The homes can be grouped into nine style categories. The number of styles in each category and examples of ones common in the Midwest are in Table 18-1.

Sources of information on style include: Harrison, Henry S and Leonard, Margery B. *Home Buying: The Complete Illustrated Guide,* and, Harrison, Henry S. *Houses,* Chicago: National Association of Realtors, Realtors National Marketing Institute, 1980, pp96-124.

Roof Types

To identify exterior style, you need to recognize types and arrangements of the roof, windows, doors, structural features, and construction materials. Common roof types are in Fig 18-1.

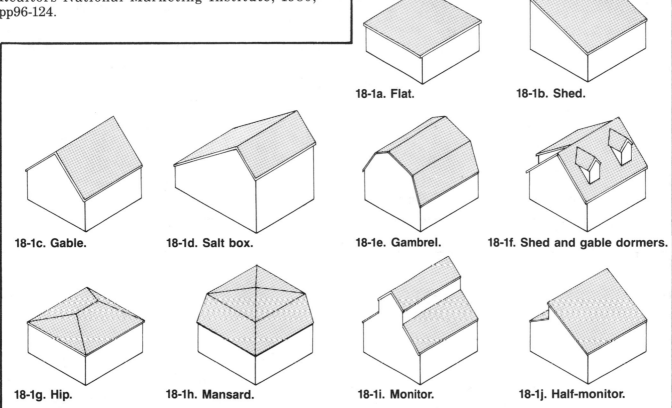

18-1a. Flat. 18-1b. Shed.

18-1c. Gable. 18-1d. Salt box. 18-1e. Gambrel. 18-1f. Shed and gable dormers.

18-1g. Hip. 18-1h. Mansard. 18-1i. Monitor. 18-1j. Half-monitor.

Fig 18-1. Roof types.

Table 18-1. Exterior housing styles.

Category	No. of styles	Example of some styles
Colonial American	15	Cape Cod Colonial, Log Cabin Colonial, New England Colonial, Southern Colonial, Dutch Colonial
English	6	Cotswold Cottage, Elizabethan/Half Timber, Tudor, Regency, Georgian
French	4	French Provincial, French Normandy
Swiss	1	Swiss Chalet
Latin	2	Spanish Villa, Italian Villa
Oriental	1	Japanese
19th Century American	17	Gothic Revival, Victorian Italianate, Eastlake, Queen Anne, Brownstone Row Houses, Monterey, Western Stick, Mission Style, Shingle Style
Early 20th Century American	5	Prairie House, Bungalow, Adobe, International Style
Post WW II American	7	California Ranch, Functional Modern, Solar House, Mobile Home, Plastic Houses

18.2

Window Styles
Window types are in Figs 18-2 and 18-3.

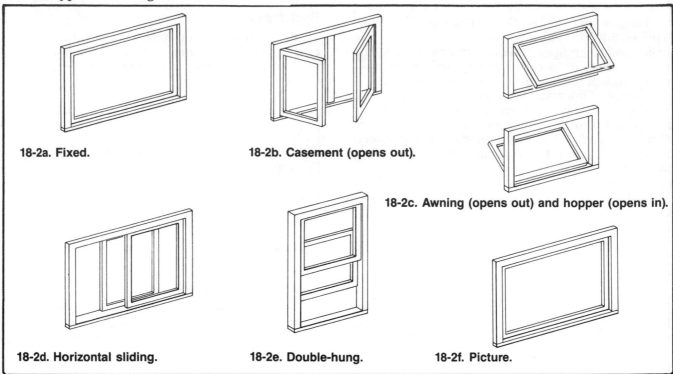

18-2a. Fixed.

18-2b. Casement (opens out).

18-2c. Awning (opens out) and hopper (opens in).

18-2d. Horizontal sliding.

18-2e. Double-hung.

18-2f. Picture.

Fig 18-2. Window types.

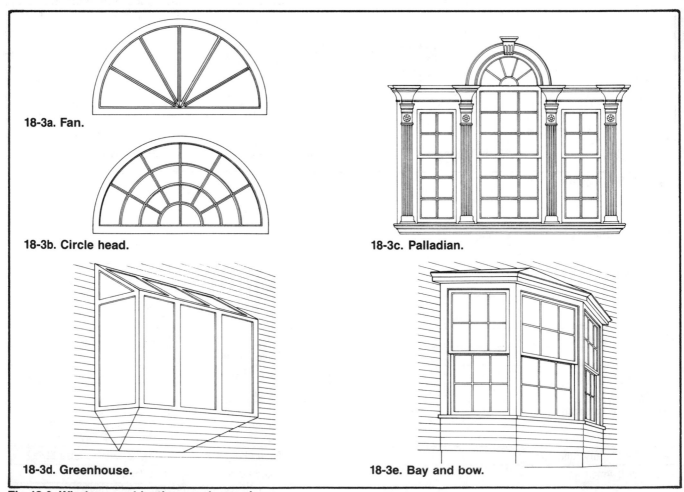

18-3a. Fan.

18-3b. Circle head.

18-3c. Palladian.

18-3d. Greenhouse.

18-3e. Bay and bow.

Fig 18-3. Window combinations and groupings.

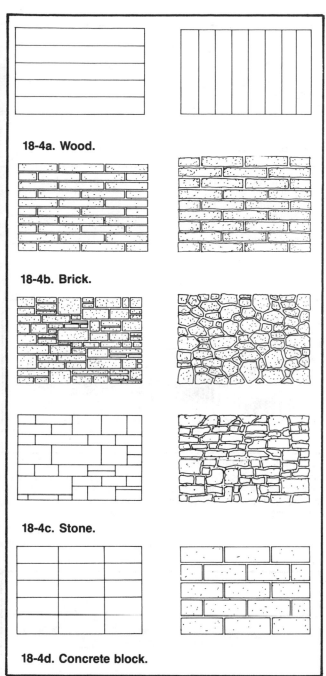

18-4a. Wood.

18-4b. Brick.

18-4c. Stone.

18-4d. Concrete block.

Fig 18-4. Siding materials.

Siding Materials

Siding provides pattern (horizontal, vertical, or unit elements), texture (smooth or rough), color (paint, stone, or brick), etc. See Fig 18-4.

Brick usually has a standard pattern, but brick size changes scale. Brick can be smooth or rough and have uniform or varying color. Vary pattern with mortar joint treatment and color with tinted mortar.

Stone can be coursed or random. Coursed stone looks smoother and has a horizontal emphasis. Cut stone can be smooth or rough; uncut stone (rubble) is usually rough.

Concrete or tile masonry can be laid in varied patterns and with different tooling in the joints.

Housing Styles

The appearance of balance is achieved with symmetrical (formal) or asymmetrical (informal) ar-

rangement of structural elements. The Cape Cod colonial, Fig 18-5, and the New England colonial, Fig 18-6, show symmetry: all elements are of equal weight and are equally spaced from the center of the design.

Fig 18-5. Colonial American—Cape Cod Colonial.
Simple versions of the Cape Cod were the earliest homes built by American colonists. It usually had 1½ stories and a steep gable roof. Double-hung windows were equal distances from the centered front door and chimney (symmetrical balance). A modified Cape Cod was popular in the 1920s and 1930s.

Fig 18-6. Colonial American—New England Colonial.
This large, roomy house was generally rectangular, with 2½ stories, side or rear wings, and a gable roof. Windows, door, and chimneys were typically symmetrical.

Fig 18-7. English Elizabethan or half timber.
This style was developed in England during the reign of Queen Elizabeth (1558-1603).

Fig 18-8. French Provincial.
This style shows perfect formal balance. It has 1½ to 2½ stories and has a high, steep hip roof.

Fig 18-9. 19th century American Eastlake.
Three-dimensional ornamentation characterized this style; many parts resemble furniture legs and knobs. They were multistory, asymmetrical, rectangular, and had an open front porch.

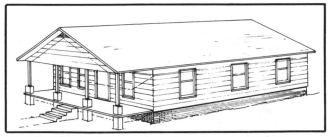

Fig 18-10. Early 20th century American bungalow.
This style of the early 1900s had many regional variations. A wide front porch (often glassed in) was characteristic. The roof was hip or gable, sometimes with a gable on the main house and a partial hip roof on the porch.

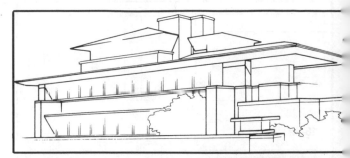

Fig 18-11. Early 20th century American prairie house.
A long, low roof line, continuous rows of windows, and a plain exterior distinguished this style. Frank Lloyd Wright designed for the physical and psychological needs of the residents, with emphasis on space organization. His impact on housing in the Midwest, West, and world wide was greatest in the first half of the 20th century. An example is Robie House, Chicago 1909.

Fig 18-12. Split level.
Since the early 1950s, the split level has gained in popularity. Designed for sloping sites, the living, dining, kitchen, and entry areas are usually at grade level with the bedrooms one-half flight up. The raised portion of the basement is more useful than in the typical one-story house.

Fig 18-13. Raised ranch (split entry or bi-level).
In the early 1960s, the whole basement was raised for useful living space. Only minimal space was reserved for utilities and storage.

19. CONDITION OF EXISTING CONSTRUCTION

This book emphasizes space arrangement and use in a house. After you are satisfied that the house being considered meets your space needs, evaluate its condition.
- Hire a qualified house inspector. Look in the phone book or ask a real estate firm for the names of local inspectors.
- Make an inspection yourself using the following checklist.

Exterior Construction

The following appear to be in acceptable condition:

		Yes	No
Foundation	Walls are straight	___	___
	Cracks have not opened up	___	___
	Mortar joints are sound or easily repaired	___	___
Siding	Edge or end grain of composition siding is not swollen from moisture	___	___
	Paint is not peeling	___	___
Windows	Storm windows are not cracked or broken	___	___
	Screens not torn	___	___
	Putty on prime windows in good condition	___	___
	Glass not cracked or broken	___	___
Gutters	Firmly attached to house	___	___
	Not rusted through on inside	___	___
Downspouts	Firmly attached	___	___
	Splash blocks or extensions at discharge	___	___
Fascia	Not rotting behind gutter	___	___
Roofing	No missing or curled shingles	___	___
	No erosion of material in valleys and between shingle tabs	___	___
Roof vents	Flashing in good condition	___	___
	Caulking around pipes okay	___	___
Chimney	Flashing in good condition	___	___
	Mortar joints sound	___	___
	Bricks not scaling	___	___
Insulation	Adequate and dry in the attic	___	___
	Adequate in sidewalls	___	___

Interior Construction

The following appear to be in acceptable condition:

		Yes	No
Basement	Sump pump works	___	___
	No evidence of flooding or dampness	___	___
Floors	Hardwood in good condition	___	___
	Vinyl not cracked or worn	___	___
	Carpets clean and serviceable	___	___
Walls and ceilings	No excessive cracking	___	___
	No stains from water leaks	___	___
	Paint or paper satisfactory	___	___
Windows	Finish in good condition	___	___
	Wood not rotting	___	___
	Operating mechanisms satisfactory (locks, sash cords, pulleys, cranks, weatherstripping, etc.)	___	___
	Storm windows operate easily	___	___
Patio doors	Double pane glass does not show air leaks, and	___	___
	Aluminum frames have thermal breaks (Hard to tell in mild weather.)	___	___
	Good locks	___	___
	Door and screen roll easily	___	___
	Has a storm door	___	___
Doors	Hardware in good condition	___	___
	Deadbolt lock	___	___
	Weatherstripping okay	___	___

Utilities

The following items have been checked:

		Yes	No
Heating and AC	Burners are clean, no rust	___	___
	Cabinet is not rusty	___	___
	Filter is easily accessible	___	___
	AC condensate drain is not clogged	___	___
Water heater	No accumulation of rust scale in the bottom	___	___
	Pilot and burner flames blue	___	___
Plumbing	Water flow and pressure satisfactory	___	___
	Faucets operate and do not drip	___	___
	Water closet refill valve does not leak	___	___
	Drains and traps do not show signs of leaks	___	___
Electrical	Service entrance is at least 100 amp rating	___	___
	Old home has been rewired	___	___
	Number of circuits and outlets is adequate	___	___
	Light switches are convenient	___	___
	Closets have lights	___	___

20. SELECTED REFERENCES

There are many sources of additional information on house planning. Some suggestions follow. Mentioning companies by name is for information and does not imply endorsement.

Local Sources

Local businesses are good sources:
• Builders and contractors.
• Banks, credit unions, and building and loan companies.
• Materials suppliers, lumber dealers, and utility and appliance retailers.
• Architects.

Bookstores and libraries have magazines and books. Many magazines have useful articles, illustrations, feature issues, and addresses for manufacturers.

Examples of publishers with series of books are listed here—your librarian or book dealer can furnish others.
• Meredith Corporation (Better Homes and Gardens Books), Locust at 17th, Des Moines IA 50336.
• Time, Inc. (Time-Life Books), Alexandria VA 22314.
• Lane Publishing Co. (Sunset Books), 80 Willow Road, Menlo Park CA 94025.
• Hearst Corporation (House Beautiful Home Interest Books), 1700 Broadway, New York NY 10019.

Agencies and Organizations

The National Electrical Code (NEC) is an accepted guide for safe electrical installations and is the basis for all electrical codes in the United States. *The National Electrical Code Handbook* has the code and explains its requirements. It is published by the National Fire Protection Association, Batterymarch Park, Quincy MA 02269.

Most cities have electrical, plumbing, and construction codes. Check your city, county, or state regulations during planning, **before you build.**

Housing and energy information are available from county, area, and state Cooperative Extension Service offices. Most have sample house plans for studying options and can help you get large scale plans to help with construction.

Almost every state has an energy office or energy education program where you can get information, and every state has several governmental agencies that can supply housing information. Some agencies have offices in many cities and towns, such as:
• State department of public health (water and waste disposal systems).
• Farmers Home Administration (financing, minimum standards).
• Federal Housing Administration (financing, minimum standards).

• Colleges and universities (general information, referrals to appropriate agencies or professionals).
• County offices of the Cooperative Extension Service in your state.
• Building inspection and code officials (requirements, limitations).

Request a list of useful housing publications from:
• Small Homes Council-Building Research Council, University of Illinois, One East St. Mary's Road, Champaign IL 61820.

Midwest Plan Service and its cooperating universities (addresses listed on the inside front cover of this handbook) offer several publications that are useful to home planners:
• *Private Water Systems Handbook,* MWPS-14, tells homeowners and farmers who get their water from private systems how to plan a new system or correct problems in an existing one and how to operate and maintain private water systems.
• *Home and Yard Improvements Handbook,* MWPS-21, tells how to plan and build home storage and numerous yard improvements. Adaptations for a wheelchair home and other construction topics are also discussed.
• *Onsite Domestic Sewage Disposal Handbook,* MWPS-24, is a guide to planning, designing, installing, and maintaining a private sewage treatment and disposal system.
• *Farmstead Planning Handbook,* MWPS-2, tells how to lay out a farmstead and how to handle drainage, snow and wind, etc.
• *Farm and Home Concrete,* MWPS-35, helps you buy and use ready-mix concrete—quality, quantity, placing, and curing.
• *Solar Greenhouses for the Home,* NRAES-2, is a guide to designing a new greenhouse or to retrofitting an existing greenhouse for use as a sunspace, a season extender, or for year-round plant production.
• *Home Storage of Fruits and Vegetables,* NRAES-7, helps homeowners adapt areas in and around the home for cold storage of fruits and vegetables.
• *Burning Wood and Coal,* NRAES-23, is a guide to using wood and coal for home heating.

Handicapped Housing Information

Organizations and rehabilitation specialists offer information, ideas, and assistance. Only a few sources are listed here.
• Easter Seal Research Foundation of the National Easter Seal Society, 2023 W. Ogden Ave., Chicago IL 60612.

- Access for the Handicapped, 1012 14th St. N.W., Suite 803, Washington DC 20005.
- Accent on Living, P.O. Box 700, Gillum Road and High Drive, Bloomington, IL 61701.
- Paralyzed Veterans of America, 801 18th St. N.W., Washington DC 20006.
- Registered occupational therapists or other rehabilitation specialists.
- Engineers, architects, or contractors experienced in barrier-free housing.

Trade Associations

Trade associations are groups representing many manufacturers of a given type of product. They have literature to help you use their members' products wisely. Six of the many associations are listed here as examples of organizations dealers can refer you to. Write the associations for a list of publications.

- Portland Cement Association, 5420 Old Orchard Road, Skokie IL 60077.
- American Plywood Association, P.O. Box 11700, Tacoma WA 98411.
- Western Wood Products Association, 1500 Yeon Building, Portland OR 97204.
- Southern Forest Products Association, Box 52468, New Orleans LA 70152.
- National Association of Home Builders of the U.S., 15th and M Sts. N.W., Washington DC 20005.
- Manufactured Housing Institute, 1745 Jefferson Davis Hwy., Suite 511, Arlington VA 22202.

21. INDEX